THE
PREACHER'S PAPERBACK
LIBRARY

The Preacher's Paperback Library
Edmund A. Steimle, Consulting Editor

Preaching
on the
Parables

DAVID M. GRANSKOU

FORTRESS PRESS • PHILADELPHIA

Library of Congress Catalog Card Number 74–165512

ISBN 0–8006–4011-X

3039H71   Printed in U.S.A.   1-4011

To Charlotte,

A Parable in Love

ABOUT THE
PREACHER'S PAPERBACK LIBRARY

The renewal of the church in our time has touched many aspects of parish life: liturgy and sacraments, biblical and theological concern, the place of the laity, work with small groups. But little has been said or done about the renewal of the church in the pulpit.

The Preacher's Paperback Library is offered in the hope that it will contribute to the renewal of the preaching ministry. It will not stoop to providing "sermon starters" or other homiletical gimmicks. It will, rather, attempt to hold in balance the emphasis which contemporary theologians and biblical scholars lay upon the centrality of proclamation and the very practical concerns of theological students and parish pastors who are engaged in the demanding task of preparing sermons of biblical and theological depth which also speak to the contemporary world.

To that end, the series will provide reprints of fundamental homiletical studies not presently available and contemporary studies in areas of immediate concern to the preacher. Moreover, because the study of sermons themselves can be of invaluable help in every aspect of the preparation of the sermon, volumes of sermons with introductory notes will appear from time to time. The sermons will include reprints of outstanding preachers in the past as well as sermons by contemporary preachers who have given evidence both of depth and of imaginative gifts in communication. It is our hope that each volume in The Preacher's Paperback Library, prepared with the specific task of sermon preparation in mind, will contribute to the renewal of the preaching ministry.

For preaching, one of the most fascinating elements of the synoptic Gospels is the parables of Jesus; and some of the scholarship which most productively assists the preacher in his interpretation of Scripture has been in this very area. David Granskou has added to that wealth of scholarship by providing us with a useful handbook in the interpretation of the parables. It will be of great value for the preacher when used in conjunction with the recent works on the parables, referred to in his essay, by Jeremias, Linnemann, and Via. Granskou provides us first with a review of parable interpretation from Jülicher down through these more recent scholars. Then he treats thirty-one of the parables briefly, with reference to the interpretations given by Bultmann, Beare, Jeremias, Linnemann, Via, and others. The author makes his own contribution to contemporary scholarship by stressing the element of humor in the parables and by emphasizing their prophetic character. Preachers and students interested in being faithful to the thrust of the parables of Jesus will find this book a useful addition to their basic library.

EDMUND A. STEIMLE

Union Theological Seminary
New York, New York
Trinity, 1971

CONTENTS

Introduction: THE LONG SHADOW OF PARABLE   1

One: THE HISTORY OF PARABLE INTERPRETATION   8

1. The Marcan Theory of Parable   8

2. Adolf Jülicher (1857–1938)   10

3. Corrections to Jülicher   21
   Rabbinic Scholarship   21
   Form Criticism   24
   Eschatological Interpretation   28
   Literary Criticism   35
   Prophetic Interpretation   41

Two: WORKSHEETS ON THE PARABLES   55

1. The Parable of the Two Debtors—
   Luke 7:41–43   58

2. The Parable of the Evil Spirit's Return—
   Matt. 12:43–45/Luke 11:24–26   61

3. The Parable of the Sower and/or the Soils—
   Mark 4:1–9/Matt. 13:1–9/Luke 8:4–8   62

4. The Parable of the Patient Husbandman—
   Mark 4:26–29   65

5. The Parable of the Weeds and the Wheat—
   Matt. 13:24–30/Thomas 57   68

6. The Parable of the Mustard Seed—
   Mark 4:30–32/Matt. 13:31–32/
   Luke 13:18–19   71

7. The Parable of the Leaven—Matt. 13:33/
   Luke 13:20–21/Thomas 96   72

8. The Parables of the Treasure and the Pearl—
   Matt. 13:44–46/Thomas 109 and 76   73

9. The Parable of the Net—Matt. 13:47–48   76

10. The Parable of the Unmerciful Servant—
    Matt. 18:23–35   78

11. The Parable of the Good Samaritan—
    Luke 10:25–37   79

12. The Parable of the Friend at Midnight—
    Luke 11:5–8   83

13. The Parable of the Rich Fool—
    Luke 12:16–21/Thomas 63   84

14. The Parable of the Barren Fig Tree—
    Luke 13:6–9   85

15. The Parable of the Choice Places at the
       Banquet—Luke 14:7–11   86

16. The Parable of the Tower Builder and the
       King Contemplating a Campaign—
       Luke 14:28–32   87

17. The Parables of the Lost Sheep and the Lost
       Coin—Luke 15:1–10   90

18. The Parable of the Elder Brother—
       Luke 15:11–32   95

19. The Parable of the Unjust Steward—
       Luke 16:1–7   98

20. The Parable of the Rich Man and Lazarus—
       Luke 16:19–31   99

21. The Parable of the Unjust Judge—
       Luke 18:1–8   102

22. The Parable of the Pharisee and the Tax
       Collector—Luke 18:9–14   104

23. The Parable of the Generous Employer—
       Matt. 20:1–16   106

24. The Parable of the Two Sons—
       Matt. 21:28–32   108

25. The Parable of the Wicked Husbandman—
Mark 12:1–12/Matt. 21:33–46/
Luke 20:9–19/Thomas 65   109

26. The Parable of the Great Supper—Matt. 22:
1–14/Luke 14:16–24   111

27. The Parable of the Doorkeeper—
Mark 13:33–37/Luke 12:35–38
(also Matt. 25:14–15b)   115

28. The Parable of the Servant Entrusted with
Supervision—Matt. 24:45–51/
Luke 12:42–46   118

29. The Parable of the Ten Maidens—
Matt. 25:1–13   119

30. The Parable of the Talents—Matt. 25:14–30/
Luke 19:12–27   121

31. The Parable of the Last Judgment—
Matt. 25:31–45   124

The Long Shadow
of Parable

PARABLE IS THE EXPERI-
ence of comparison. It is as old as man laughing at
his reflection in the pool, and it is as old as the Genesis
account of creation which sees man in comparison—in
the image of God. The first language seen on the
caves of prehistoric man was comparison by means of
pictures. Simile, metaphor, allegory, similitude, fable,
and parable are the grammar and style of man's insatia-
ble urge to compare. Comparison is in fact the rhythm
which brings joy, learning, sorrow, pain, repentance,
new life.

To study the parables of Jesus is not merely to
engage in a narrow religious or literary effort. "The
kingdom of God is like"—this formula introduces more
than a literary form. Jesus' parables bring together two
different kinds of human experience. What is remarkable is not the words or style of the language, but the
striking nature of the comparison itself. The sandwich-
ing together of realities from different planes of living
tends to add perspective and new texture to our experience. The success of Jesus' parables often rests on

surprise. We are taken off our guard by the progression of the story. The parable leads us from very familiar and understandable aspects of experience to a sudden turn of events or a remarkable comparison, and in consequence we reflect on life in a new and more meaningful way. Thus parable, comparison, is part of human experience.[1]

We owe a great deal to modern scholars like Adolf Jülicher for pointing out certain stylistic features of Jesus' parables. It was he who saw that Jesus was making *one* point with simplicity in each of his parable stories. And this is a necessary warning. Jesus is doing more than taking over a story-form from his environment. Finding the one point, distinguishing between parable and allegory, or parable and similitude, are all laudable efforts. Nevertheless, analysis of the parables of Jesus must begin and end with their truly human mystique—the mystique of man's learning by bringing things together for comparison.

As a form of teaching, Jesus' use of parable requires the acceptance of comparison, which is an inductive and open-ended form of communication and learning. Comparison says, "If A is like B, we can learn about B by what we know about A." Jesus was suggesting that we know a great deal about secular or everyday life, and if we see the connection of the secular to the sacred we could have our understanding of religion expanded. Parable as comparison thus expands our religious expe-

1. See M. Foss, *Symbol and Metaphor in Human Experience* (Princeton, 1949). Also other literature and a survey of the subject in *Religion im Geschichte und Gegenwart*, 3rd ed., vol. 2, cols. 1614–15 (hereinafter cited as *RGG*).

rience, but we must be very careful not to reduce such meaning to abstract dogmatic statement. The parable form is used to widen horizons. One of the dangers with which this book will struggle is the temptation to package up a neat moral out of each parable. The dynamics of the parable form is so much richer than mere terse, interpretive moral statements. The meaning of the parable is always to be experienced in more than dogmatic categories. The whole mystique of comparison is always there.

Parable consequently provides a springboard for reflection. It functions to turn people on, to unwrap truth (rather than to wrap it up), to cause wonder and laughter. Because of its habit of expressing truth in abstractions, modern Western thought finds it strange to encounter stories and word pictures as vehicles for religious truth. We like pictures, but we still desire to reduce the picture to a sentence. Impressionistic painting and sculpture is a case in point. We are not happy with a work of art until we get its name, and have a brief explanation of its meaning by the artist or some noted critic. The recent debate over the Picasso sculpture in downtown Chicago is an example. Was the statue a bird, a lady, a man, or something else? One of the politicians pronounced, "It's a she!" But Picasso remained silent; the statue spoke for itself.

The parables of Jesus have their own speech also. Comparison breaks the rational limits of classroom language. It has instincts and feelings which spring out of life itself. As life is simple, the parable is simple. As life is full of complexity, parable beckons us on to explore mystery and religion. This dialectic of the simplicity of the truly profound and the profundity of the truly simple is part of the makeup of parable. This dialectic is crucial if we are to deal with the delicate question of avoiding both over- and under-explanation in the interpretation of Jesus' parables.

To avoid both over- and under-explanation is an issue which has troubled many who have attempted to teach the parables or to learn from the many excellent interpretations now available. I have found that even outstanding students can read these excellent studies and still not catch the style of parable expression with its quickness and zest. It generally takes a classroom discussion to bring about the moment of comprehension. We might raise the question, "Can the meaning of the parable be stated in one sentence?" Jülicher said that the parable had one point of simplicity and still took 641 pages to explain these simple points!

So we stand at the beginning of our study of the parables of Jesus mindful of the paradoxical nature of our task. We must point out both the profundity and the simplicity which lie at the heart of the act of comparison which we know as parable.

We also ought to be mindful of the special authorship of the parables in the New Testament. They are the parables of Jesus. In surveying the total collection of Jesus' parables in relation to those of others who in his day used this form of teaching, we can see that he was a master of the form. This raises the additional question of the relation between the artist and his work. Most artists do not offer explanations of their artistic achievements. This is true not only of visual artists, painters and sculptors, but also of poets, writers, and men in the wisdom tradition who often insist that their words must stand alone so that the reader or listener is forced to participate in the creative act. Some New Testament parables have interpretations; many do not. Did Jesus supply these explanations to his parables? The consensus of current scholarship is that the parables are forceful enough to stand alone without explanation. If this is so we then have to deal with the mystery of Jesus' intention as well as with the mystery of the parable itself. Jesus calls us to examine the dynamics of his stories in order that we might come to know the secret of his proclamation. Indeed, the parables, as a tradition of sayings in the New Testament, furnish us with an excellent example of the meaning of Jesus' ministry and person. We can see our Lord as a man of keen observation. His statements have an open-ended quality which leads us to constant reflection and to an awareness of the greatness of the one who is behind the words.

An initial reaction to the unique mystique of Jesus' parables might imply that the ordinary mortal has no right to approach this holy of holies with his own act of personal interpretation. For almost two thousand years an allegorical understanding of the parables did in fact discourage the layman from looking at the simple drama unfolded in the stories. The fathers of the church stood as high priests of interpretation. Augustine, for example, furnished elaborate allegorical keys to many of the parables which were then taken as nearly normative interpretations. Luther endeavored to free the Bible from this captivity to the doctors of the church, but he was not totally successful. In the nineteenth and twentieth centuries a new high priest of interpretation appeared—the biblical scholar, who usually holds a doctorate in biblical or near eastern studies, and who is generally identified with some school of interpretation such as form, redaction, or literary criticism. The purpose of modern biblical studies is to make the Bible clear to the reader, but the mass of scholastic tools with which it works often obscures this intent.

Jesus' parables do not need to call forth this high priesthood of interpretation. There is more to the parables and more to Jesus than reading the fathers of the church or modern commentaries. Jesus' parables must be understood in relation to his person, his incisiveness and compassion, his wit and wisdom, his concern to call his people back to God.

The present study comes out of my own personal experience in teaching the parables to a wide variety of audiences—seminary students, parish pastors, university students, laymen and women in congregations. They all needed an exposure to technical points of modern interpretation, but that alone was never enough. As I reflected on the problem of interpretation with these groups it dawned on me that the mystique of Jesus' parables was not uncovered merely by elaborating on the scholarly studies now available. What is missing in these studies? For one thing, they hardly ever bring into focus the element of humor or wit found in Jesus' parables. So I have been led to struggle for a proper understanding of these elements and what they might do to clarify the vitality of Jesus' expression. It now seems strange that something so obvious has been neglected in scholarly works on the subject for such a long time. Perhaps it violates scholarly seriousness to speak about humor.

Here I am forced to a criticism of much recent scholarship concerning the parables. It is not so much that many scholars have taken an incorrect direction as that they have narrowed the issues to that which is purely technical. Three hitherto neglected factors will emerge in our study—*wit, wisdom,* and *prophecy.* Our conviction is that no interpretation of the parables of Jesus can achieve true technical competence until it rises above that which is merely technical to the level of that which is genuinely human.

ONE

The History of
Parable Interpretation

IT IS NOT THE PURPOSE
of this book to engage in an extensive history of the
exegesis of Jesus' parables. We shall content ourselves
with an overview of the role of certain key stages in
that long history.

1. The Marcan Theory of Parable

It is one of the ironies of biblical scholarship that the
accepted understanding of the parables was controlled
for close to nineteen hundred years by a theory of
allegory whose origins are obscure. Most of the parables
of the New Testament, however, in fact occur without
allegorical embellishment. It is in Mark 4:10–20 in
connection with the parable of the soils that we find
a suggestion that the parables of Jesus are obscure and
need interpretation. The origin of these verses is complex. V. 10, linked with vv. 13–20, comes from a
source which maintains that the disciples needed, and
were supplied with, an allegorical key. Vv. 11 and 12
come from another source and assert that Jesus' disci-

ples understood what Jesus was about but that it was the outsiders who did not and would not understand or repent. Some have suggested that this second saying concerning the disciples who understand and the outsiders who do not, might best be seen in a setting independent of the parables. This view would then go on to show that this contrast between the disciples and the outsiders was inserted by the first evangelist in keeping with the "messianic secret" of his Gospel. What is important for us in this whole section of Mark is the insistent pointing to the obscurity of the parable. In vv. 33–34 the evangelist again records that Jesus needed to explain his parables.

It would be unfair to insist that these statements in Mark were alone responsible for the long centuries of allegorical understanding. In the ancient world allegory was a popular form of interpretation and was applied as a matter of course to the Old and New Testaments in many ways. Thus, even without the Marcan passage it would have been likely that the allegorical method would have been applied to the parables. Still, when it is specifically suggested that Jesus employed allegory, there is sure to be added attention paid to that category. In addition, this scriptural reinforcement kept the parables in the bondage of allegorical interpretation long after it was abandoned as a method of understanding other parts of the New Testament. Even more interestingly, I can press the point one step further on the basis of my own personal experience in teaching parables. I have found that in respect to the parables students may be ready to give up allegory in all cases save that of Mark 4. To me this says that even if we accept the fact that Jesus may not himself have been responsible for the allegorical interpretation of that passage, the force of the interpretation remains. We will have to take this question up in more detail when we come to the exposition of the parable of the soils in the second part of this study.

The quite inescapable fact is that the one New Testament instance of allegorical interpretation, Mark 4:10–20, 33–34, was enough to throw the weight of subsequent exegesis in that direction—for close to two thousand years! Here is evidence of the difficulty we face in reaching new understandings of Scripture once an "official" or semiofficial line of interpretation has been established.

2. Adolf Jülicher (1857–1938)

This is the name that looms large in any history of the exegesis of Jesus' parables. It is to his credit that he decisively broke with the dominant form of allegorical exegesis. An excellent example of German academia at the end of the nineteenth and the beginning of the twentieth century, Jülicher grew up in the heyday of historical-critical scholarship. The great German exegete Bernhard Weiss (1827–1918) had a great influence on him encouraging a careful attention to grammatical and historical exactitude. After six years in the parish Jülicher was called to be professor at the University of Marburg. He occupied that post from 1888 until retirement in 1923. In his retirement he continued his New Testament research, although from 1925 to his death he was almost totally blind.

It was as a young pastor of twenty-nine years that Jülicher entered his mark in the history of New Testament studies. The first edition on the general meaning and purpose of parables, *Die Gleichnisreden Jesu*, came out in 1886. He reworked this and added a detailed exegesis of individual parables in 1899. Apparently his hope was further to rework this study, but sickness and other duties kept him from his goal. Thus in 1910 he came out with a second unaltered edition of the 1899 work dedicated whimsically to Mark 4:26–29, "The Parable of the Seed Growing Secretly." He was aware that more work needed to be done on the material and hoped that others would correct and carry forward the task.

It is often stated that the major concern of Jülicher was to press for a "one-point" principle of interpreting parables which would also reject allegorization. This is true, but it is an abstract way of looking at the question. As a result of this simplified abstraction, many lesser scholars subsequently have engaged in the rather shabby sport of one-upmanship. In fact it might lead us to suspect that not all of the critics of Jülicher have read Jülicher.

It is instructive to begin by reading the preface to the second edition of Jülicher. There he apologizes for not rewriting his whole study, seeing it as too big a task. However, he does lay down the direction which he would take in such a rewriting. In that discussion he clearly states that the most important section in his book is chapters 2 and 3, the chapters which deal with the essence and purpose of parable. He also suggests that he would take the text, Mark 4:1–25 and 33–34 as the springboard for his discussion.[2] Thus it is clear that Jülicher sees the discussion about parable in Mark 4 as the chief problem in coming to a proper understanding of the text. His comments are most helpful because it shows Jülicher functioning as an exegete dealing with specific texts. The one point is never an abstract principle; it is rather the whole or single impression which the audience must have had when they heard Jesus speak the parable of the man sowing the seed. Likewise, his use of the term "allegory" must be understood in the sense of esoteric explanation, as it is developed in Mark 4:10–20 and 33–34.

Taken in this context of Mark 4 Jülicher sets allegory and parable in opposition to each other. He wishes to define this difference from the vantage of how the speaker wishes to speak with his audience. In respect to allegory he points out the intent of the speaker is to hide a truth rather than to reveal it, to divide the audience into two groups rather than to unite it, to mystify rather than to convince. Allegory speaks a code language to an esoteric group, and thus excludes those in the circle outside this small group. The outsiders cannot understand. Sometimes even the insiders cannot understand until they have an explanation given to them.

Jülicher goes on to define the parable in the context of Mark 4:3–8. He terms this a parable. As such the

2. See Adolf Jülicher, *Die Gleichnisreden Jesu* (Tubingen, 1910), 1:4.

story moves within the context of everyday life. It does not shy away from the humble or the sinful in life. From this base its purpose is to clarify the noble and divine, to show opportunities and laws in the kingdom of God, to move from the level of the known to the level of the unknown. Jülicher would claim that anyone in Jesus' audience would be able to understand what he was talking about. Thus parable does not make a distinction in the audience between those who know and those who do not know.[3] As Jülicher reads vv. 3–8, there is a clear message which needs no interpretation outside the words of the story itself. He also asserts that vv. 10–20 and 33–34 are not the words of Jesus, but of the evangelist Mark. For him one has to make a simple and radical choice: with either Jesus or the evangelist, but not with both. Jülicher's concluding plea for this decision is filled with the rhetoric of high emotion. He speaks about the need to place Jesus in high respect and not take diamonds out of his eternal crown of glory. If we are to avoid taking the gems out of Jesus' crown we must begin by at least taking a few pebbles out of the huge wall of tradition which imprisons Jesus and his words. We do this with the act of confession. That is, to acknowledge that the parables of Jesus are a simple form of speech in spite of anything which Mark or the other evangelists might say.[4]

A second step in Jülicher's argument is to compare the parables in the synoptic Gospels with those in other places. He judges the form of the synoptic para-

3. Ibid., p. 118.
4. Ibid., p. 148.

bles to be different from those found in the Fourth Gospel (John 15:1–8) and the Shepherd of Hermas. He characterizes the similitudes in the Shepherd as cold, trite, and abstract, contrasting the warmth, depth, and concreteness of those recorded in the synoptics. Again, he is not doing this in an absolute way as though every parable in the synoptics can be seen as the product of a religious genius. In fact he debates against this type of understanding, even going on to admit that some of the parables there are defective *(mangelhaft)* in substance. However, allowing that observation, the parable tradition as a whole is seen by Jülicher as a remarkable collection of sayings which go back to Jesus.[5]

We may now review the main point of Jülicher's reasoning. He is in the first instance arguing from a concrete set of texts. He sees that the overall impression of the parables of Jesus as recorded in the synoptics is different than that of similitudes found in the Shepherd of Hermas or the allegory of the Gospel of John (John 15:1–8). He also sees that the parabolic interpretation in Mark 4:10–20 and 33–34 overlooks the simplicity and clarity of the very parable it sets out to explain. He then continues his concrete approach by arguing from the historical point of view: how would the original audience respond to the parable story? His answer is, they would understand it.

At this point a digression is in order—to evaluate a frequent criticism of Jülicher. He is often charged with being too abstract in his presentation of the single-

5. Ibid., pp. 23–24, and 117. In the first citation is the comparison of the synoptic parables with those of the Shepherd of Hermas, and in the second with the Johannine allegory of Christ as the true vine.

point interpretation as opposed to the allegorical interpretation. Further, he is sometimes accused of not
having been interested in penetrating behind the evangelists to the historical situation of Jesus himself.[6] I do
not find these criticisms fully helpful, for they seem to
be criticizing a subpoint in Jülicher as though it were
the main point. Thus the contribution of the man is
made to appear formalistic and allows later generations
of readers to misunderstand him and thus to escape the
force of his challenge.

The so-called one-point method of interpretation is
only the abstract side of the main point. What Jülicher
really is stressing is the reaction of those who first heard
the parables. *They* had no technical instruction as to
how to hear Jesus. They simply came and were struck
by what he had to say. He spoke as one who had an
authority greater than that of scribe or Pharisee. What
they heard was so forceful and clear that the stories
were remembered without any special interpretation.
When interpretation was later added it tended to forget
this original force of communication. Thus the one-
point interpretation has the feel of the parable in mind,
the story as forceful communication. Jülicher is calling
us back to the intensely human situation in which the
parable was first uttered.

6. Joachim Jeremias, *The Parables of Jesus,* rev. ed. (New York:
Scribner, 1963), pp. 19–22. Jeremias seems to give no credit to Jülicher
for seeing the radical difference between the evangelist and Jesus. Perhaps this is best understood as rhetorical overstatement. Likewise, Wil-
helm Michaelis, *Die Gleichnisse Jesu* (Hamburg: Furche Verlag,
1955), pp. 14–16, seems to suggest that the distinction between parable and allegory is purely theoretical, a point which again seems overly
polemical in view of the express intent of Jülicher.

In my mind parable exegesis has not been the same since Jülicher, and even those who seem to reject his method have been influenced by it. No one in recent times has engaged in a massive allegorical interpretation which has won any wide acceptance. I choose to suggest that those of us who live after Jülicher are at most engaged in making technical corrections of his method; in the main we follow his central argument, even if we are not willing to acknowledge it. Of course, we shall also want a place in the sun, so we shall try to lay bare some totally new and unusual point of departure which others have missed. The fact remains, nevertheless, that Jülicher's central place in the history of parable exegesis cannot be ignored, nor can the concrete and central issue he raised be avoided in any subsequent technical refinements. Jülicher is the watershed in the history of parable interpretation. Geraint Jones is correct in suggesting there is a "before and after Jülicher" in this history.[7] We would go even a step further to point out that so far his central thesis has not been upset. What we have seen is a series of arguments with some of the technicalities of Jülicher's position. The history of the interpretation of the parables has been advanced only by way of technical corrections of Jülicher. In our survey[8] we shall attempt briefly to summarize a representative, not exhaustive, number of these corrections. They can be classified as follows: rabbinic

7. Geraint V. Jones, *The Art and Truth of the Parables* (London: S.P.C.K., 1964), pp. 3–41. It is in addition striking that Jones would make this concession to Jülicher, knowing of his very sharp criticism of him later in this study.

8. See below, pp. 21 ff.

scholars (Paul Fiebig, Paul Billerbeck); form critics (Martin Dibelius, Rudolf Bultmann); eschatological interpreters (C. H. Dodd, Joachim Jeremias); literary critics (G. V. Jones, Dan Via); and the criticism of prophetic irony (the present author).

Before we consider these "corrections," let us show how Jülicher laid out the technical side of his position. This demonstration will serve as a kind of defense of Jülicher's main thesis, his lasting contribution to the history of parable interpretation.[9]

Jülicher's formal argument is contained in his chapter on the "essence" of the parables of Jesus.[10] Here he indicates that the two basic forms of parabolic speech are "simile" *(Vergleichung)* and "metaphor," a distinction made familiar long ago by Aristotle. This is a distinction between *stated* and *unstated* comparison. Both forms compare, but they differ in their *stated* versus *unstated* manners of expression. "She walks into the room like a horse," is a stated comparison, the use of the word "like" making the comparison a simile. If we say, referring to the same person, "The horse walks into the room," we suddenly are dealing with a metaphor, an unstated comparison. In both cases we have the same old clumsy girl, but with metaphor we are more

9. Cf. the article on parable by Friedrich Hauck in *Theological Dictionary of the New Testament,* Gerhard Kittel, ed., Geoffrey W. Bromiley, trans., 6 vols. (Grand Rapids, Mich.: Eerdmans, 1964–69), 5:744 ff., especially p. 753, n. 66 where Hauck asserts that Jülicher's permanent contribution was his fundamental distinction between parable and allegory.

10. Jülicher, *op. cit.,* pp. 25–118. For an excellent summary, see Jack Dean Kingsbury, *The Parables of Jesus in Matthew 13* (Richmond, Va.: John Knox Press, 1969), pp. 1–3.

subtle about our expression. If we use this expression at a party, some who hear our slur may not understand. There is one in every crowd who never understands the metaphor: "What horse? I don't see any horse." But if we shift to the direct simile, "She walks into the room like a horse," it is clear what is meant. Jülicher describes the simile as a direct form of speech *(eigentliche Rede)*, metaphor as an indirect form of speech *(uneigentliche Rede)*.[11] From these simple units of speech, Jülicher works out a schematic classification:

	Stated Comparison	Unstated Comparison
1. The simple unit	Simile	Metaphor
2. Expanded unit	Similitude	
3. Story—expansion to express a truth	Fable, or parable in narrow sense	Allegory
4. Story—expansion to change action	Example story	

Stated comparisons begin with a simile, a figure of speech joining two things in an explicit way, generally with the term "like." The similitude is an expanded simile comparing two thoughts or sentences. An example would be, "As a hart longs for flowing streams, so longs my soul for thee, O God" (Ps. 42:1). Jülicher is clear concerning what he calls the *tertium comparationis,* the point of coincidence. The hart is not to be compared to the soul in all respects, but only at the single point where its thirst for water corresponds to

11. Kingsbury, *op. cit.,* p. 2, translated a little differently: "The metaphor is non-literal speech *(uneigentliche Rede),* i. e. it says one thing but means another; the simile is literal speech *(eigentliche Rede),* i. e. each word is to be taken at face value; the metaphor demands an interpretation and remains a mystery outside of its context, the simile admits of no interpretation because it is always self-explanatory."

the soul's thirst for God. This comparison is stated, the term used is "as." It is clear that a comparison is being made.

The next form of stated comparison is the fable or parable in the technical sense. Fable is not to be confused with an animal story. Here also we encounter the narrow sense of parable, an imaginary story relating to an event in such a way that a general truth can be drawn.

Not all stories of this type, however, are for the purpose of drawing out a general truth. There are example stories which aim at the listener and serve as a mirror. In effect one is to see the action of the story as something to emulate. Luke 10:30–37 (the good Samaritan), 12:16–20 (the rich farmer), 16:19–31 (the rich man and Lazarus), 18:9–14 (the Pharisee and the publican) are taken as example stories.

It should be noted that the distinction between parable and example story is sometimes unclear. Some stories of this type can function either way. It is always important to test the intent of the speaker: does he wish to state a general truth (parable) or confront the listener (example story)? We will go into this question further in our discussion of individual parables.

The other basic type of comparison is that which is unstated. The smallest unit of this is the metaphor. A metaphor is a figure of speech joining or comparing two things by implication. "The ship plows the sea," is an example. It suggests, but does not state, that a ship is like a plow. The previous example we used, "The horse walks into the room," may obviously not be about a horse at all. It may concern a person of dubious grace.

Take this type of unstated comparison and put it into story form and the result is an allegory. Jülicher was of the opinion that this type of communication was impossible to understand unless one possesses a more or less authoritative interpretation as in the allegorical theory of the evangelists. It was, moreover, Jülicher's contention that this was not inherent in the nature of the parables themselves.[12] This judgment is based on a literary observation that the parables of Jesus appear as real-life stories with a great deal of warmth, emotion, drama, and realism. Allegory tends to lack this unitive appearance because its attention is focused on the little unstated comparisons in every sentence. An interpreter can overinterpret a parable by considering it an allegory, but this need not destroy the unitive character of the narration. Because the parable is a stated comparison its style of expression is straightforward while that of the allegory is more devious. In sum, an allegory calls for speculation, a parable calls for a judgment on one specific question.

As now presented, Jülicher's conclusions are rather abstract. But at its deepest what comes forward is a picture of Jesus as a straightforward person whose sayings are clear in expression. We have the image of Jesus as the simple Galilean preacher, an image which Jülicher shared with the nineteenth-century biblical research. This is hardly an image presupposed

12. See Jülicher, *op. cit.,* p. 49.

today,[13] but it should be pointed out that Jülicher himself suggested in the preface to the 1910 edition of his work that advances in biblical scholarship would ultimately call for this type of revision.

3. Corrections to Jülicher

Rabbinic scholarship. In 1903 the Norwegian scholar C. A. Bugge came out with an attack against Jülicher and his "radical" commentary on the parables.[14] More important, however, was the work of Paul Fiebig who did a detailed study of the rabbinic parables in comparison with those of Jesus.[15] What Fiebig criticized turned out to be Jülicher's dependence on Aristotle for his model of parable and allegory. This was, he asserted, not a historical way to proceed. Jesus was closer in style to the *meshalim* of the rabbis than to Greek literary theory. Thus it follows that the rabbinic style of parable is a good point of entry to the parables of Jesus.

The rabbinic *mashal* was not a rigid form. It could be a parable, an allegory, or a mixture of the two— an allegorical parable or a parabolic allegory. Fiebig argued that Jesus came into a country where the religious tradition was familiar with the parable form, and that he would use this form in a way which was

13. So N. A. Dahl, "Gleichnis und Parabel," in *RGG,* vol. 2, col. 1618.

14. C. A. Bugge, *Die Hauptparabeln Jesu* (Giessen, 1903), vol. 1.

15. Paul Fiebig, *Die Gleichnisreden Jesu im Lichte der rabbinischen Gleichnisse des neutestamentlichen Zeitalters* (Tübingen, 1912). For others who have followed in this line of attack see Kingsbury, *op. cit.,* p. 4, n. 14.

conventional and understandable to his time. This means that we should anticipate occasional variations in Jesus' style of parable.

What this does in correcting Jülicher is to introduce more freedom for the interpretation of individual parables. It is not helpful to make a prior assumption that all the parables in the New Testament must have the same dynamics. One of the contributions that this type of correction will make on the present study is to make it more situational in character. It is not helpful to categorize in advance all the parables as to their form. This would be prejudicing the case before completing a serious study of the individual dynamics.

Fiebig has also shown that the distinction between simile and metaphor may hold in small units, but not in the larger units. Thus parable and allegory as extended examples of the two types of speech charted out by Jülicher may not be all that different. There is a sense in which a parable is an allegory with one point. Even if we do not want to make every detail in the story stand for something it might be legitimate, for example, to see God as the master or the father in a story. The rabbinic tradition of parable certainly used such standard symbols.

This is a very attractive criticism of Jülicher. Who could know the Jewish Jesus better than the Jewish rabbis? It is like wanting a Russian guide to show one around Moscow. But there are difficulties in such a request as soon as one realizes that the guide might be a pawn in someone's plan to propagandize. The question which must be asked of Fiebig concerns his major purpose. Is he studying the relationship between Jesus and the rabbis for its own sake, or to attack the position of Jülicher? He must offer a broader-based study of the rabbis which deals with more issues than whether there is allegory in the rabbinic parable tradition. It is therefore well critically to examine the conclusions of Fiebig.

The first question to raise concerns Jesus and the rabbis. Was Jesus a rabbi? This is a complex issue to which a yes and no answer is appropriate. Jesus was a teacher, but his authority was not that of the scribes and the Pharisees. The Jesus in the Gospels sometimes engages in a rabbinic type exegesis, but this often appears in highly edited texts. The deeper question is one of Jesus' originality. Even if he was influenced by the rabbinic tradition of parable speech he also brought his own original touch to the parable form. All creative people have a way of standing above their tradition, and the movement away from the allegorical style *may* have been one of the hallmarks of Jesus. I say *may* simply to indicate that Fiebig's method cannot come to grips with the vital question of the originality of Jesus or the extent to which he used allegory.

We must also remember that Fiebig belonged to a school of biblical research which was prone to make extreme statements about the whole of the New Testament and its rabbinic background. More recent study has reminded us of the difficulty of making too many affirmations about the rabbinic theology of the first century because all the texts are from a much later date. The sources about Jesus are in many instances as close or closer to the first century than the sources about the rabbis. Fiebig's mixed form of parable may be suffering from a kind of transmission alteration.

The value of Fiebig is not that he refuted Jülicher, but that he showed the need for further research on the nature of parable and resisted drawing the categories of parable, allegory, and example story too tightly.[16]

Form criticism. Of the form critics we shall deal briefly with Martin Dibelius and Rudolf Bultmann since their early works concerning the synoptic tradition fit into the history of parable interpretation. Both of these men came to their use of the form-critical method by way of the historical criticism of the nineteenth century. They were thus both in basic sympathy with the aims of the historical-critical scholarship practiced by Jülicher. Both also had to deal with the polemic raised by Fiebig concerning the work of Jülicher. Dibelius seems to have been more attracted to Fiebig's arguments than Bultmann, the latter's stay with Jülicher at Marburg perhaps accounting in part for his sharp attack on Fiebig in defense of Jülicher. Whatever the reason, we see in these two form critics a refinement and development of the insights of Jülicher's classic research.[17]

Dibelius' work began with the first edition in 1919 of his book on form criticism.[18] In this work he offered

16. See Kingsbury, *op. cit.,* p. 7. Jeremias also resists the idea that parable was a narrow concept or story form. See Jeremias, *op. cit.,* p. 20.

17. A valuable introduction to form criticism is Edgar V. McKnight, *What Is Form Criticism?* Guides to Biblical Scholarship (Philadelphia: Fortress Press, 1969). Also in the same series, Gene M. Tucker, *Form Criticism of the Old Testament* (1971).

18. For the English translation of the second edition see Martin Dibelius, *From Tradition to Gospel* (New York: Scribner, n.d.), pp. 246–58.

a classification of Jesus' stories, and puzzled over the questions of the one-point interpretation, and the role of allegory in the parables. He seemed to come to the conclusion that some parables had two points, and others had allegorical elements, a conclusion which in his judgment required an alteration in Jülicher's position. He made one further contribution to the problem. While Jülicher pointed out the tendency of the church in its tradition to allegorize the parables, Dibelius pointed to a similar tendency to moralize them. He asserted that almost the whole of the parable collection had been changed by this tendency, and that in the process the dynamics of the original situation were very often lost. This was an advance of considerable significance for the form-critical method, laying bare as it did a second major factor in the alteration of the original meaning of parable.

In 1921 the first edition of Rudolf Bultmann's *The History of the Synoptic Tradition* was published, a volume which advanced the work of form criticism on the parables.[19] Bultmann paid especial attention to the unspoken rules of parable narration. He was careful to note that the parable type of story was not a self-consciously composed piece of literature, but a work of folk wisdom. He laid down ten rules which stressed the brevity and simplicity of the form.[20] One of the most important of these rules was that the point of the parable most often came at the very end, an insight of

19. For the English translation, Rudolf Bultmann, *The History of the Synoptic Tradition* (New York: Harper & Row, 1963), pp. 166–205.
20. See ibid., pp. 188 ff., or the summary in Kingsbury, *op. cit.,* p. 8.

considerable help in any effort to uncover the dynamics of the parable form.

Of equal value is Bultmann's distinction between *general* and *specific* meanings. As an example, he pointed out the general meaning of the parable of the sower (Mark 4)—courage in the face of discouragements. However, just what the precise situation of the parable was is unknown, and therefore we are hard put to find the specific meaning. It is, of course, the work of interpretation to come as close to the specific meaning as possible.

Perhaps the most important observation and suggestion of Bultmann is to be found in his refutation of Fiebig's proposition concerning the presence of allegory in the rabbinic tradition. He expands on his refutation by offering what seems to be a better definition of the difference between parable and allegory. The crucial category for Bultmann is that of "transference of judgment," an element present in parable and lacking in allegory. One is attracted to a story from a sphere of life which is not religious, and there encouraged to make certain judgments. Suddenly these judgments are transferred to a religious problem.[21] This transference clarifies the religious issue. It is precisely this which is missing in allegory, for the purpose of allegory is not to clarify but to puzzle. One is robbed of insight unless one knows the key to the story. A further fact to note is that allegory is not as likely to lead to existential judgment as is the transference in a parable.

---

21. See Bultmann, *op. cit.*, pp. 198–99.

It is the task of form criticism to discover the point at which the transference of judgment takes place, both in a general and a particular way. An example would be the parable of the sower. Just as the sower has difficulties in his sowing, but finally discovers success in the harvest, so in the religious sphere there is final success. Here a transference of judgment reveals the general point of victory in spite of discouragement. However, the specific discouragement and the particular victory are unclear. Form criticism has as its task the reconstruction of the original situation out of which the parable arose. Bultmann, to be sure, is not always certain that one can penetrate back to the original setting; nevertheless, such remains the goal. While Jülicher to a certain extent had a similar concern, it is the form critic who presses with greatest force for the original meaning in the ministry of Jesus. Thus the work of Bultmann remains even today a wealth of information for the student who is seeking out the primary from the secondary. This distinction is accomplished by rigorously noting the editorial process which underlies the setting of the parable as well as by uncovering which of the parables might have originated with Jesus, which with Jewish sources, and which with the early church. Bultmann finds, to be sure, that many of the parables represent the morality of Judaism or the viewpoint of the church and therefore cannot represent the original preaching of Jesus.

To sum up: form criticism, especially as practiced by Bultmann, works to clarify the basic insights of Jülicher concerning the nature of parable as distinct from allegory, and its hope is to separate primary from secondary readings in the parable tradition.

Eschatological interpretation. It is in a way surprising that eschatology was not more evidently an element in the corrective work of form criticism. To be sure, Bultmann did note the importance of the eschatological in his understanding of what was genuine in the tradition of Jesus.[22] However, it was C. H. Dodd and Joachim Jeremias who attempted consistently to carry out this aspect of New Testament scholarship into parable interpretation.

The earlier contribution of Johannes Weiss and Albert Schweitzer was to put an end to the liberal image of Jesus as a Jewish preacher of righteousness. This they did by showing that the central proclamation of Jesus was the inbreaking of the kingdom of God, which was in fact a term taken out of Jewish eschatology, a term which pointed to a new age in history.

The basic result of this insight when applied to the parables, especially by Dodd and Jeremias, has been to remove more decisively from the parables any moralistic interpretation. Thus an additional criticism of Jülicher's moralistic approach comes to the fore, especially opening the category of example story to additional suspicion. When the eschatological element is given its place the basically dynamic quality of the stories comes into fuller view.

---

22. See the end of his treatment of parable, *op. cit.,* p. 205: "We can only count on possessing a genuine similitude of Jesus where, on the one hand, expression is given to the contrast between Jewish morality and piety and the distinctive eschatological temper which characterized the preaching of Jesus. . . ."

The move away from allegory and moralism also involves an attempt to arrive at the original meaning of parable in the ministry of Jesus. Both Dodd and Jeremias place great stress on this. They feel that the early church often had difficulty understanding the point Jesus was trying to make, and by striving to uncover original situations and meaning their work represents a continuation of Jülicher.

One of the most helpful results of Jeremias's work is his formulation of *laws of transformation*. Jeremias observes that the factors which are involved in changes of meaning can be grouped into ten laws or principles of transformation. Underlying these laws is the contention that the parables underwent change when they were passed down in the oral and later in the written tradition of the church. His rules are as follows:

1. When the parables were translated into Greek there were changes due to the difficulty of translating certain expressions into the new language.

2. Translation of the stories from Palestinian to Greek and Roman culture also involved shifts of expression. Actions in the stories representing grief, joy, prayer, legal action, etc. were often in need of some alteration in the new cultures.

3. Embellishment of the stories also occurred. This could produce subtle shifts of meaning.

4. Passages of Scripture and folk-story themes have also been introduced.

5. Parables originally addressed to opponents have been later applied to the Christian community—with resultant shifts of emphasis.

6. There is also a shift to hortatory application.

7. There are also reorientations to missionary concerns caused by the delay of the parousia.

8. Details in the parables have also been allegorized so as to bring in new doctrinal and moral issues.

9. Parables with similar themes have been collected together so as further to homogenize meaning.

10. New settings and generalizing conclusions produce qualifications of meaning.

Jeremias sees the sum total of these shifts as being of great significance. Implicit in his evaluation is the feeling that Jesus' own interpretation of the parables is paramount for us.[23] Jeremias feels that it is all too easy to suppress valuable and important insights from both Jesus himself and the earliest tradition because of abstract concerns for the unity of the New Testament. While he would not deny all of the interpretive effort of the early Christian community he does see the need to be aware of those occasions when that community misunderstood or flattened out the more dynamic proclamation of Jesus and the first generation Christians. The New Testament includes interpretive material which at times comes from as late as the second generation of the tradition.

From this analysis Jeremias proceeds to an exposition of the parables with major reference to the eschatological perspective. He sees ten major themes in the parables:

1. Now is the day of salvation.

2. God is merciful to sinners.

23. See Jeremias, *op. cit.,* pp. 11–114, for full discussion. Also Jeremias, *Rediscovering the Parables* (New York: Scribner, 1969), pp. 17–88, for a somewhat briefer discussion of the same issue.

3. The great assurance of God's victory.

4. The judgment of God as imminent.

5. It may be too late to avert God's judgment.

6. The challenge of such an hour demands clear action.

7. Description, demand, and comfort in the discipleship realized in Jesus Christ.

8. The way of suffering and the exaltation of the Son of man.

9. The consummation and final judgment of God.

10. Jesus' parables in action.[24]

These themes are grouped around the secret of the kingdom, namely, the dawning of the messianic age. Thus the basic message for Jeremias is that with Jesus the blind see, the heavy burden of guilt is removed, the lepers are cleansed.[25]

In summary there are two main points in the argument of Jeremias. First, the attempt to recover the meaning of the parables in the light of the ministry of Jesus. Second, the classification of meaning by themes revolving around the secret of the kingdom of God (Mark 4:11). This secret is not an allegorical key, but rather the eschatological fact of the new age.

It is also interesting to note how Jeremias has been criticized because of his attempt to return to the original meaning of the parables at the time of Jesus. We have here a return to the old question of Jülicher, that is, the desirability of the quest for the original meaning of Jesus. Many feel that to discern the difference be-

24. See Jeremias, *The Parables of Jesus,* pp. 115–229, and a summary in Jeremias, *Rediscovering the Parables,* pp. 89–179.
25. Jeremias, *The Parables of Jesus,* p. 181.

31

tween the dynamics of the story and the interpretation stated in a particular Gospel is to split hairs. There are those who feel the need to resist the historical-critical process of interpretation because of its implied primitivism. Such primitivism seems to insist that the earliest part of the tradition is automatically the best and all which follows is an inferior development. By his concern for the meaning of parable in the life of Jesus Jeremias offers a value judgment in favor of the superiority of the earliest part of the tradition. He has a great deal of confidence that it is possible to get back to the words of Jesus in the parables. Interpretation per se is a negative value for Jeremias: little is done in his study to distinguish between good and less helpful applications.

One of the tasks before us then is clearly the matter of interpretation. We shall have to see where an interpretation is correct, extends the parable helpfully into a new situation, turns its whole meaning in a new but unrelated direction, or essentially subverts the original meaning. It is perhaps correct to assume that Jeremias left that task to the reader of his study. This may be possible in the German situation where his work would be well enough known to allow the reader to draw some independent conclusions. In the American situation, however, this is not the case. To study the parables on the basis of his book leads many to view his study as though it were strictly an academic exercise. Even Jeremias's shorter summary of the parables, *Rediscovering the Parables,* leads the reader to downgrade the interpretive elements found in the Gospels and the tradition.

The later interpretive additions are always seen as a potential, and often an actual threat to the meaning of Jesus. Further, the meaning of Jesus is most often held to be the meaning most worth preserving. Failing to discriminate between the interpretations may be Jeremias's basic scholarly shortcoming. The unevenness of the interpretive elements added to the parables surely needs further scrutiny. We shall have to take each interpretation and uncover its value even when it lacks a base in Jesus' own ministry.

In spite of these criticisms, however, there is need to commend the work of Jeremias. To turn to the original setting does not require an arbitrary judgment that the oldest is the best. Traditions after all do not just happen. They come into being because of a remarkable origination. The search for the oldest stage of the parables is not whim. It is rather a search for that which is at the font of the Christian tradition. This does not mean the whole of the parable collection in the New Testament necessarily has to go back to Jesus. It does, however, go back to something. There is a great deal of originality and beauty in what comes to expression in the parables; there is nothing quite like them in the literature of the early church. This suggests a creative person behind the parables. The best candidate for authorship is Jesus. This proposition can be debated and might appropriately be so debated in another context, but for the purposes of this study it is enough to give credit where it is due. Jeremias has rendered invaluable service to our understanding of parable by stressing the need to look back as far as possible in an effort to recover the force and point of the original parable, perhaps as Jesus originally delivered them. Serious criticism of Jeremias has to be at some other point than his "primitivism."

It is striking indeed that so few have criticized Jeremias's stereotyping of the message of the parables around the theme of the kingdom of God. Perhaps this is due to the acknowledged service of Weiss and Schweitzer in destroying the liberal image of Jesus. We can of course agree: one of the important themes which Jesus did proclaim was that of the radical invasion of the kingdom of God. But, is this all he preached about? It seems historically improbable for Jesus to have had only one theme with which to carry out his brilliant ministry. In respect to the parables we raise the same question. Do they all have to be about the kingdom of God? This seems to be a constriction of meaning before exegetical investigation. It is better to have an open mind about the question of an overarching theme.

Furthermore, it is important to raise the question whether the parables actually have only one point. Many have criticized Jeremias for following Jülicher on this. There is no point in denying the essential insight of the one-point theory of interpretation. What Jeremias and Jülicher really have in mind is the unity of impact which is found in the parables of Jesus, and the object of their criticism has been the way some of that unity has been destroyed by later interpretation. But have they stated the one-point theory correctly? Jeremias's ten themes are stated as declarative sentences, propositional in nature.

Now thoughts and propositions can be stated without stories. A great deal is added when these points are made in a story form. The story introduces an element of *nonverbal communication*. For instance, the three stories about God's mercy to sinners in Luke 15 stress different things because the stories are different. These different emphases are more important than Jeremias has been willing to acknowledge. It will be our task to bring out the combination of thought and feeling in interpreting individual parables. In stressing the nonverbal elements, to be sure, there will have to be care not to return to some type of allegory. We shall have to concentrate on the image impact and the realization that such communication is open-ended and impressionistic.

Literary criticism. New Testament studies have a way of revolving around certain basic issues. One such issue is that of the literary form of the New Testament. Form criticism is one way of stating this concern, a discipline in which literary form is related to the historical question. How did a certain form evolve? What was the use of a particular literary form in the community? Was the form part of a liturgy, a confession, a debate, or some other community problem? As we have seen, the historical interest in literary form has been with us since the time of Jülicher.

Now it appears that a new literary interest is developing in particular relation to the parables. This interest sees the parable as a literary form which has artistic importance quite apart from historical questions. This type of interpretation is often called literary criticism, a term used to suggest that the literary form is worthy of study on the aesthetic level. The aesthetic form is seen as having an impact on the reader in its own right.

Such concerns are certainly not totally new in New Testament studies. However, since the discovery of Adolf Deissmann and others that the language and the style of the New Testament is that of the "common" first-century man, literary criticism has tended to be out of favor. New Testament studies in the first half of the twentieth century were strongly influenced by the assertions of Deissmann and others who held that the New Testament was not to be classed as formal literature. Form criticism went in the same direction by speaking of the Gospels as products of the primitive Christian community. In the last few years, however, there has been a revival of interest in the discipline of literary criticism as it relates to the New Testament. For one thing there have been advances in the field of literary criticism which in themselves warrant attention. Further, the idea that the Gospels were simply pericopes strung together in a haphazard way has not been maintained. Form-critical studies have analyzed the final process by which sayings and stories were collected into a Gospel: What did the final author or redactor have in mind as he put his finished product together? Some of the concerns leading to the final product were surely literary. So we are back full circle. Attention to form led to the historical quest behind the form, which brought us to the author and his literary aims.[26]

26. For a clear introduction to this discipline, see William A. Beardslee, *Literary Criticism of the New Testament,* Guides to Biblical Scholarship (Philadelphia: Fortress Press, 1970) and in the same series, Norman Habel, *Literary Criticism of the Old Testament* (1971).

Thus in the past few years many New Testament scholars have developed an interest in the aesthetic side of the New Testament because their historical studies of the texts have not led them far enough. They see that a study of the history of a text does not always lead to the consideration of meaning. G. V. Jones is the first in recent times to press for the use of literary criticism in the study of the parables, having put forth his views in his work, *The Art and Truth of the Parables*.[27]

Jones represents a type of British scholarship which sees limitations in form-critical or historical studies because they tend toward historicism, that is, toward a concern for the past for its own sake. There needs in this view to be a wider interpretation of the parable which also speaks to the issues of today. We are not in a position to enter into the general hermeneutical discussion of the relation between ancient meaning and modern application, but we would like to point out that at times it appears that Jones is arguing for a return to the kind of parable study dominant before Jülicher. It is of no great value to turn to a literary-critical method as though it could replace historical study; but it is of value to see what the literary method might do to aid or expand historical investigations. If, therefore, I see value in the literary-critical method it is not at the expense of historical studies.

The contention of Jones that the story form of the parable has its own message is of helpful importance. It is not enough for us to recreate the historical meaning of the parable apart from its literary structure, because its

27. See above, p. 16, n. 7.

literary structure is part of the message of the parable. Speaking of tales Jones says, "They are, moreover, continually creative because, not being limited by the formal accuracy of the letter, they enable the spirit, the creative and religious imagination, to speak freely."[28] What Jones asserts is that the form of the parable will go on speaking through the ages. Our particular interpretation is accordingly valid even if it might be different from that of Jesus. From a different angle, I would further maintain that a story form presents the subtlety of emotion. A sentence which appears in a conceptual framework is relatively free from emotional overtones, but the same sentence in the framework of a story is likely also to be filled with emotional meaning. It is from this side of the picture that literary criticism, as advocated by Jones, aids our study of the parables. Emotional statement never settles for a concept because a concept is a closed statement. A story, like a picture, is an open statement in the sense that one can look at it many times and each viewing offers a new experience in meaning and feeling.

A second scholar who has made an important argument in favor of the literary understanding of the parables is Dan Via.[29] He criticizes the historical approach of German scholarship by contending that such a method ignores the aesthetic nature of the parables and "annuls their aesthetic function."[30] Furthermore,

28. Jones, *op. cit.,* pp. 128–29.
29. Dan O. Via, Jr., *The Parables, Their Literary and Existential Dimension* (Philadelphia: Fortress Press, 1967).
30. Ibid., p. 24.

he argues that the historical method also ignores the human element, and leaves the parable addressing situations of the past with "nothing to say to the present."[31]

Via maintains that the parable has a language of its own which is powerful enough to propel meaning forward: "Therefore, in interpreting the parables for contemporary understanding the texts offer possibilities for translation that are not altogether dependent on the conscious awareness of the author and the original audience."[32] Here is an extremely important question. What happens when a man speaks? He may say precisely what he intends to, he may say more, he may say less. What is the duty of the interpreter? Is he speaking to words or to the man who utters the words, or to both? In dealing with this issue we must recall that historical-critical interpretation wishes to penetrate to the meaning of the speaker as he talks to the original audience.

The scope and purpose of this study do not allow us to work through the whole hermeneutical question involved here. We can only comment that Via seems to be overreacting to the concern of historical interpretation for what the original speaker had in mind. If Jesus had no particular meaning in mind when he spoke one of the parables we are engaged in a pointless enterprise. After all, the church has remembered the parables because Jesus spoke them—the parables of the New Testament are important primarily because they are the parables of Jesus.

31. Ibid., p. 22.
32. Ibid., p. 32.

Does one have to be against historical interpretation in order to use literary interpretation? We view the interest in literary criticism with something less than the evangelistic fervor of those who feel it to be *the* method to replace strictly historical interpretation. We use literary criticism of the parables not to sidestep historical issues but to face them. We also maintain that historical meaning is not to be set in opposition to universal meaning. Any universal meaning always finds part of its validation in relation to the historical situation.[33]

The most interesting use made of literary criticism by Via is the classification of some parables as "comic" and others as "tragic." His understanding of comedy is in the broad sense of plot "that moves upward toward the well-being of the protagonist and his inclusion in a desirable society."[34] His understanding of tragedy involves the sense of plot "moving downward toward catastrophe and the isolation of the protagonist."[35]

Via classifies the following parables as comic: the workers in the vineyard (Matt. 20:1–16); the unjust steward (Luke 16:1–9); the prodigal son (Luke 15:11–32). The tragic parables are: the talents (Matt. 25:14–30); the ten maidens (Matt. 25:1–13); the wedding garment (Matt. 22:11–14); the wicked tenants (Mark 12:1–9); the unforgiving servant (Matt.

---

33. Via himself is not unwilling to submit himself to some historical considerations even though the language previously quoted would lead one to that conclusion. For more moderate statements see pp. 184 ff. in his study.

34. Ibid., p. 145.

35. Ibid., p. 110.

18:23–35). It is clear that not all the parables in the New Testament lend themselves to this classification, but at points the method does work. We must therefore keep in mind the possibility of using plot to uncover part of the meaning in the parables. Among the many elements of our study, the art form of the parable is not to be disregarded.

Prophetic interpretation. We now come to the central point of our study. While the points of view which have been discussed have offered much of value for the interpretation of the parables, not enough has been made of the parable tradition in the Old Testament, especially those parables which are found in 2 Samuel. True, many scholars refer to those parables, but few have looked with sufficient care into the emotional and situational dynamics which are involved in them. For too long the scholarly debate has centered in the question of whether the parables have only one point or whether they can be given allegorical meaning. This type of analysis keeps us from looking into other aspects of parabolic speech.

The tradition found in 2 Samuel is most revealing for our study. The language of this tradition reveals a certain type of dynamics between the prophet and his audience. The study of these parables also gives us a fuller picture of what Christ was about in his ministry. He was certainly more than a prophet, but this ought not to blind us to the intensely prophetic elements within his proclamation. Very little has been said about these elements in Jesus' parables. This may be accounted for by the fact that the early church so quickly made these stories into allegories and morality statements.

A key part of prophetic interpretation which has received little or no treatment in modern studies of the parables is the element of humor. Humor seems to be a category which is forbidden! We know, however, that Nathan used a type of humor when he spoke his parable to David. This absence of discussion concerning the role of humor in the parables says a great deal about the false seriousness of modern New Testament scholars and modern preachers. We can be so serious about pursuing meaning that we forget the need for the perspective of humor in the quest of truth. Studies on the parables—like those of Dodd, Jeremias, Via, Linnemann—have for some strange reason not proven to be as helpful to many of my students as I had anticipated. I have recently come to the realization that because humor has not been a part of these studies they have been unable to present totally convincing and lively cases. My more recent experience has been that for many preachers, students, and laymen the element of humor has become the most important key to a revived understanding of the parables of the New Testament.

We know of Jesus as a man acquainted with grief, but he could also laugh at the human scene. The delightfulness of the parables consists in part in this light touch. There is a laughter which leads to repentance and change just as there is a cry of sorrow which leads to new life.

A second item, after humor, in prophetic interpretation is open-ended communication. Open-endedness in prophetic speech means that the utterances of the prophet are designed to elicit response, not unalterably to pronounce truth. In Jonah we see this in a most graphic way: when the people repented the prophecies made against the city were not carried out by God. The point of such parables is not to teach a dogmatic or moral truth which is not otherwise known, but rather to set in motion a process of reflection on life. This openness also lays bare a great deal about the emotional situation of the prophet and those he is prophesying against. The prophet is not simply against them; he is with them. The audience against whom the prophet is speaking possesses the capability of providing some of the answers to what is in question.

A third item, part of a prophetic interpretation, is the situational aspect of parabolic communication. This is not to take up the old debate about whether parables possess only a past meaning related to a given historical situation or also a general meaning for all ages. Such a debate requires a radical either/or in response to the question of historical versus existential interpretation. Situational interpretation means, rather, that the communication is practical rather then theoretical in intent. In one sense this does militate against "general meanings." One cannot disregard the situation out of which the parable arose without distorting the meaning. Yet the message of the parable does not remain only historical. It limits the relevance of the parable by demanding that application to subsequent times and situations must pass the test of correspondence. General meanings are ruled out in an abstract sense. The contemporary meaning must be directed to a situation which corresponds to the original situation to which the parable was spoken. The parable of the good Samaritan is a good example of a parable which requires close attention to the situational question. That some interpretations of this parable have promoted Gentile pride over and against the Jewish nation shows how far afield we can go when the situational aspect is disregarded.

It is important at this point of our presentation to remember that the temptation of the exegete is to claim that his interpretation is totally new and invalidates everything which has gone before. Our "prophetic interpretation" is not the most significant advance in New Testament research on the parables, but it does claim to be an important addition to the already impressive literature on this subject. I am certainly building on the work of those who have gone before: Jülicher, Dodd, Jeremias, Dahl, Linnemann, Via, and others. My concern is chiefly to carry this work forward by pointing out the striking nature of the openness, wit, and wisdom of Jesus as he prophesies against his people in the form of the parable. It is important more closely to identify Jesus with the parable tradition of the Old Testament, especially that of 2 Samuel. We propose also to underscore how parables work in respect to the qualities of humor (generally ironic humor) and that open-endedness which creates new situations.

Föhrer has pointed out in his study of the symbolic action of the Old Testament prophets that there are only five fully developed parabolic stories in the Old Testament: 2 Samuel 12, 2 Samuel 14, 1 Kings 20:39–43, Isaiah 5:1–7, and Isaiah 28:23–29.[36] Of these, three are

36. See Kurt Föhrer, "Gleichnis und Parabel," *RGG,* vol. 2, col. 1615–16.

worthwhile studying because of their similarity to many of the parables of Jesus: the parables in 2 Samuel 12 and 14, and 1 Kings 20. The 2 Samuel parables are the best known and the most interesting from a literary point of view. That they come from the ancient document of royal succession, 2 Samuel 9–20, is also of interest. While the date of this section of 2 Samuel is under dispute it is apparently close to the time of King David himself and thus offers us a most interesting account of the origins of ancient Israelitic prophecy. Professor Maass of Berlin has argued that Nathan stands as the first historically certain prophetic witness to the Jahweh faith.[37]

Nathan's parable to David is certainly his most famous utterance.

And the Lord sent Nathan to David. He came to him, and said to him, "There were two men in a certain city, the one rich and the other poor. The rich man had very many flocks and herds; but the poor man had nothing but one little ewe lamb, which he had bought. And he brought it up, and it grew up with him and with his children; it used to eat of his morsel, and drink from his cup, and lie in his bosom, and it was like a daughter to him. Now there came a traveler to the rich man, and he was unwilling to take one of his own flock or herd to prepare for the wayfarer who had come to him, but he took the poor man's lamb, and prepared it for the man who had come to him." Then David's anger was greatly kindled against the man; and he said to Nathan, "As the Lord lives, the man who has done this deserves to

37. See Maass, "Nathan," *RGG*, vol. 4, col. 1311.

die; and he shall restore the lamb fourfold, because he
did this thing, and because he had no pity."

Nathan said to David, "You are the man. . . ."

(2 Sam. 12:1-7)

Here we find the three elements of humor, open-endedness, and situationally oriented language. Some would
like to think of the first, humor, as irony or sarcasm.
While it would not be a matter of great moment to give
up the term "humor" there seems to be some cause for
retaining the broader category. Humor has a more positive ring than irony. The purpose of keeping the more
positive sounding term "humor," is to remind us that
the prophet is not totally negative in his approach to
his people.[38] Irony is often "put down" language, and
this is not the point of the prophecy of Nathan. While
there is a strongly confrontational aspect to the parable
it is also clear that Nathan does not condemn David
outright. In vv. 13–14 it seems as though David is almost expecting total condemnation from Nathan and
God. At that point Nathan begins his speech of judgment with the assurance that God has "put away"
David's sin and that he shall not die. There is to be a
punishment, but David himself is spared the worst.

What is meant by humor? It is the ability to see the
incongruent in life. Our parable works on the principle
of this incongruence by drawing out two traits in one
person, King David. The parable itself brings out the
just side of King David, and in response to the story

38. See my article, "Prophecy and Paranoia," *Lutheran Quarterly* (Win-
ter, 1971), where I point out that a prophet is not as negative as is
often thought. Thus the prophet is not paranoid, but positive in his
declarations against his people.

he himself asserts that the man who took the lamb in the parable deserved to die and would have to make up the theft fourfold. As the just side of the king is brought out, the prophet goes on to compare the thievery of the man in the parable wth the thievery of David. But it is necessary for the king to see the incongruency himself. When he does, he moves toward confession and repentance. This is humor. The prophet may in fact be using a form of irony, but it is also clear that the king has to have sufficient humor or perspective to be able to laugh at himself. Thus the situation we are describing is one which requires humor on both sides of the communication. Both the teller and his audience must have sufficient humor for the communication to occur.

Open-endedness occurs in the situation we have just described. In an open-ended communication the speaker does not make all the steps of communication on his own while his audience waits passively for the end. Rather, the speaker lays out a situation which has an open end, and this calls on the audience to make a response of its own if the circle of communication is to be finished. In this case David makes a quick response to the parable, thus participating himself in forming the final meaning. This open-endedness has sometimes been obscured in the New Testament, but I contend that this is in fact the motive which may have been behind Jesus' use of the parable form. If so, Jesus was not out to teach a totally new moral or religious truth, but rather to engage his audiences in a situation of dialogue. This is a very important factor to remember because it suggests that the prophet is willing to accept those whom he is prophesying against: they must participate with him in seeing what needs to be changed. The point is not that they lack the intelligence or sensitivity and need to be driven to the truth, but that they rather are in need of a suggestion which will serve to activate the sensitivity and rightness which they already possess. The prophet by his open-endedness goes halfway; the hearers must go the rest of the way themselves.

It is also clear that the truth Nathan expressed is a situational one. David was aware of the general truth about stealing. What he needed to know was the direct application of such general truth to the situation of his affair with Bathsheba. Could this situational emphasis be the way to look at the parables of Jesus? If so, we have another clear reason why it is better to understand parable as prophetic rather than didactic. In David's case the parable was unmistakably specific. Nathan was not speaking a general truth to David. If he had been doing that we would have to assume that David did not know the moral truth of honesty in respect to property. Nathan would then be a figure who raised the level of moral consciousness in the court of David. We must admit that this is also on occasion the implication in the parables of Jesus. It is easy to think of Jesus as a teacher who brought us from the lower level of Jewish morality to the higher level of Christian morality.

To sum up, the genius of the parable of Nathan is found in the way David's goodness is used to uncover his evil. The gift of the parable is its use of the indirect form of communication which forced David to invest something of himself into the parable and in this way to come to an awareness of what was wrong in his relationship with Bathsheba. It was not necessary for David to be told about the general morality of the affair; it was rather necessary for him to realize through the parable how much he himself was against such action.

An equally interesting parable is the one recorded in 2 Samuel 14:1–21:

> Now Joab the son of Zeruiah perceived that the king's heart went out to Absalom. And Joab sent to Tekoa and fetched from there a wise woman, and said to her, "Pretend to be a mourner, and put on mourning garments; do not anoint yourself with oil, but behave like a woman who has been mourning many days for the dead; and go to the king, and speak thus to him." So Joab put the words in her mouth.
>
> When the woman of Tekoa came to the king, she fell on her face to the ground, and did obeisance, and said, "Help, O king." And the king said to her, "What is your trouble?" She answered, "Alas, I am a widow; my husband is dead. And your handmaid had two sons, and they quarreled with one another in the field; there was no one to part them, and one struck the other and killed him. And now the whole family has risen against your handmaid, and they say, 'Give up the man who struck his brother, that we may kill him for the life of his brother whom he slew'; and so they would destroy the heir also. Thus they would quench my coal which is left, and leave to my husband neither name nor remnant upon the face of the earth."
>
> Then the king said to the woman, "Go to your house, and I will give orders concerning you." And the woman of Tekoa said to the king, "On me be the guilt, my lord the king, and on my father's house; let the king and his

throne be guiltless." The king said, "If anyone says anything to you, bring him to me, and he shall never touch
you again." Then she said, "Pray let the king invoke the
Lord your God, that the avenger of blood slay no more,
and my son be not destroyed." He said, "As the Lord
lives, not one hair of your son shall fall to the ground."

Then the woman said, "Pray let your handmaid speak
a word to my lord the king." He said, "Speak." And the
woman said, "Why then have you planned such a thing
against the people of God? For in giving this decision
the king convicts himself, inasmuch as the king does not
bring his banished one home again. We must all die, we
are like water spilt on the ground, which cannot be
gathered up again; but God will not take away the life
of him who devises means not to keep his banished one
an outcast. Now I have come to say this to my lord the
king because the people have made me afraid; and your
handmaid thought, 'I will speak to the king; it may be
that the king will perform the request of his servant. For
the king will hear, and deliver his servant from the hand
of the man who would destroy me and my son together
from the heritage of God.' And your handmaid thought,
'The word of my lord the king will set me at rest'; for
my lord the king is like the angel of God to discern
good and evil. The Lord your God be with you!"

Then the king answered the woman, "Do not hide
from me anything I ask you." And the woman said, "Let
my lord the king speak." The king said, "Is the hand of
Joab with you in all this?" The woman answered and
said, "As surely as you live, my lord the king, one cannot turn to the right hand or to the left from anything
that my lord the king has said. It was your servant Joab
who bade me; it was he who put all these words in the
mouth of your handmaid. In order to change the course
of affairs your servant Joab did this. But my lord has
wisdom like the wisdom of the angel of God to know
all things that are on the earth."

The situation in this parable is similar to the parable of Nathan. The reader of the passage is called on to observe the humor, in which the elements of trickery and indirection are used to make the point. Absalom had fled Jerusalem because he had ordered his servants to kill his brother Amnon who had raped his sister Tamar. David was caught in a crosscurrent of emotions. While he mourned the murder of his son Amnon, he also saw the justice of Absalom's revenge. Joab, the prophet comes into the picture at this point. He wants Absalom to be brought back out of exile. He sees that David still loves Absalom (14:1), but he also knows that he cannot himself go directly to David and tell him to allow Absalom to come back from exile. His tactic is to bring David to a point where he himself will be forced to admit his love of Absalom. It is at this point that the parable is used.

The woman of Tekoa is instructed to tell the parable. Again David sees the logic of the situation in the parable and speaks on behalf of the woman who is acting for a justice which is more than simple revenge. When he does this he speaks against himself. So again, the use of the parable brings the king to speak against his own actions and thus to repent and change his ways. In v. 13 it is stated that the king had convicted himself, and further on the woman concludes her plea with a positive affirmation about the ability of the king to discern good and evil.

It is most important to see this affirmative aspect of the parable, otherwise the subtlety of the whole thing is missed. It works with the light touch of suggestion.

We do not have merely an illustration which has to be used because the listener is too dull to understand a straight moral statement. What we have is the opposite: the listener (in this case King David) has all the knowledge of good and evil necessary to act correctly. What he needs is the perspective to see how his knowledge applies in his own situation. The situational element in the prophetic speech of the parables in 2 Samuel makes them different from Aesop's fables or other morality stories told to children for the purpose of painlessly instilling ethical preachments. (At this point we must also offer a word of caution against the tendency of both Jülicher and Bultmann to see so many of the parables of Jesus as example stories.)

The writer of the document of royal succession in 2 Samuel wishes the reader to laugh with King David as he comes to a better perspective about his own life and his own actions of repentance called for by the message of the parable. By describing the king's sin the author also speaks of his nobility.

Did Jesus consciously pattern his style of parabolic rhetoric after the parables in 2 Samuel? This is a question we cannot propose to answer. We have to do with more than mere imitation. What we can examine in the parables of Jesus are the dynamics of language which come into play. What does the parable say both to those who first heard and to those who are still hearing the words? To do this we must of course use the tools of literary and form criticism as we know them. We must also be interested in the redactional changes made in specific instances. But this does not mean a simple repetition of the interpretation of others. We shall also include the prophetic vision with its humor and open-ended address to specific situations. Thus we will gain insight into what the parables of Jesus meant as well as what they mean today.

With this we launch into an interpretation of the individual parables of the New Testament. This book is a manual for preaching, and as such chooses to be brief and suggestive rather than exhaustive and exhausting. (It is hoped, to be sure, that a wider audience of both laymen and scholars will find things of interest in this study.) We need never conclude that simple brevity and scholarship cannot go hand in hand. The brevity in the comments which follow is not intended merely to popularize. If the scholar accepts the discipline of brevity he is also forced to come to the point more directly. The fact is that preachers, like laymen, no longer like to be talked down to, and scholars no longer see the necessity of weighing a volume before reading it. Let us hope merely that the worksheets that follow help all who read to move one step forward in appreciation of the wit and wisdom of Jesus who spoke and still speaks, often even through those who preach, the prophetic word to those who will listen.

TWO

Worksheets on the Parables

IT IS DIFFICULT TO KNOW how best to study the parables. They could be grouped according to a variety of criteria, but in any grouping there is an implied interpretation which may say more than is really intended. I have chosen simply to take the parables as they are found in the ninth edition of the standard Huck-Lietzmann synopsis of the Gospels.[1] I find this the easiest synopsis of the New Testament to use, though other synopses would be acceptable. In what follows the numbering of the parallels is that of Huck-Lietzmann, and all passages in question are listed for those readers who do not have parallels readily available.

To take the parables in series underlines the inductive nature of our investigation. There is as yet no grand overarching division of the parables which has won unalterable acceptance. To use a grouping along

1. Albert Huck, *A Synopsis of the First Three Gospels*, 9th ed. (a complete revision of earlier editions by Hans Lietzmann) (Tübingen: J. C. B. Mohr, 1936). The text is in Greek. The English translation is Burton H. Throckmorton, Jr., ed., *Gospel Parallels, A Synopsis of the First Three Gospels,* 2nd ed. (New York: Thomas Nelson, 1957).

the lines of a theme, furthermore, tends to discourage independent research on the text by the reader. It is, finally, difficult to make a totally satisfactory choice of parables in the New Testament because some fall in doubtful areas which may actually involve some other basic form of expression. We shall examine thirty-one parables.

In commenting on the parables we shall not rehearse everything that has been said about them, but will confine ourselves to that which is most essential. We shall endeavor both to build on the insights of scholars who have already worked on these texts, and also to show how a "prophetic interpretation" would be helpful. Naturally some parables do not lend themselves to such interpretation, and we will try to identify them. It is important to preserve a balance between our interpretation and that of others.

In the end we are hoping that the reader will gain some sense of independent judgment for himself. The eyes of the reader are the final judge as to whether or not an interpretation is helpful. Good scholarship ought not override one's reading sensibility, but rather enhance it. We hope this study will keep in front of the reader some of the following items:

1. The unity of the parable itself apart from the introductory and concluding remarks which most likely are not part of the story first spoken by Jesus.

2. The critical turn in the plot which often develops in the last sentence in the parable, and which often reverses the viewpoint of the story thus producing new insight into life and into Jesus' call to his people.

3. The fact that the early church had a variety of ways to interpret parables, and that distinctions must now be made between the methods of interpretation which are more helpful and those which obscure or confuse the meaning of the parable.

4. That there is value in the work of Jeremias, Dodd, and others in seeking the meaning in Jesus' original presentation of the parable.

5. That out of past meaning a present application can be made which ought not to be in conflict with the original intention of Jesus.

6. That it is important to study the literary form of the parable because Jesus was a great and creative person whose words are worthy of study for their beauty as well as for their historical and existential meaning.

7. That the prophetic element of Jesus' parables is to be noted along with his wit, wisdom, and ability clearly to discern situations requiring reform and renewal.

In the study of each parable we will include two sections: a reconstruction of the prophetic setting and a presentation of the prophetic meaning. These sections correspond roughly with what is sometimes called the historical meaning and the contemporary application. There is such a distinction to be made between past meaning and present translation, but one that ought not be pressed too far. The two meanings are tied together, and it is not until we get to the present meaning that the past meaning comes fully clear. There is, of course, a major debate behind this type of assertion. I can illustrate it out of practical classroom experience. Time and again I have seen students struggle with more intricate historical problems only to pause, make the translation, and come out with trite old Sunday school truisms. One then surely doubts whether the student really knew what he was doing in his pursuit of the historical meaning. Put another way, the historical meaning is what it meant, and the application is what it means. It is always necessary to understand historical meaning from the vantage of our specific time in history. Historical meaning must make sense and sense implies some type of relevance. Relevance is itself an experiential factor, and thus to express the relevance of a historical meaning is already to be on the verge of experiencing its present value.

1. Parallel 83: The Parable of the Two Debtors— Luke 7:41–43

Reconstructing the prophetic situation. We are fortunate to begin our study of the prophetic element in the parables with the present parable. Luke has clearly preserved a tradition of parable telling in which Jesus' parables originated in the specific context of a debate with the Pharisees. This can be clearly seen in Luke 15 as well as in the present instance. Was the parable first spoken when Jesus was anointed, and was the Pharisee's name really Simon? Jeremias seems to accept a historical connection between the anointing and the parable of the two debtors.[2] Bultmann has his doubts, suggesting that the account of the woman anointing

2. See Joachim Jeremias, *The Parables of Jesus*, rev. ed. (New York: Scribner, 1963), pp. 126 ff.

Jesus' feet was invented to give the parable a sense of realism.[3]

I propose not to attempt to prove whether this particular incident was the historical occasion for this parable. I would simply argue that this incident, *or a similar type of incident,* best accounts for the meaning the parable is trying to express. Jesus is not trying to make a general dogmatic point about forgiveness being the basis for love. Such a truth has long been known, even in Jesus' day. What he was doing with the parable was practical: to remind someone that his life needed to be filled with more graciousness, and that he should be less judgmental.

Luke, and his tradition, has clearly seen the need to direct the parable into the specific situation, and the setting of the anointing seems so proper that we might easily hold to the historicity of Luke 7:36–46. Jesus thus had a specific purpose with the Pharisee—not to teach him new truth, but to remind him of what he knew. V. 43 puts it, "You have judged rightly."

The truth is simple. Graciousness when given in abundance to the greatest debtor triggers a response of love. There is nothing more to it than that. The problem is, however, that we can forget this simple truth and the parable clears the air. In fact the Pharisees had rejected the majority of the Jewish populace because they were not up to the "high standards" of the Pharisees. In this parable these "high standards" are chal-

---

3. See Rudolf Bultmann, *A History of the Synoptic Tradition* (New York: Harper & Row, 1963), p. 20. Frank W. Beare, *The Earliest Records of Jesus* (Nashville, Tenn.: Abingdon, 1962), p. 99 seems to go in the same direction.

lenged when it is suggested that man's failures and need for forgiveness are intimately related to his responses of love.

The parable turns the tables on the Pharisee's judgment. The debtor and the love expressed boldly confront Jesus' society. Look for acts of love among the outcasts, not among the morally respectable! The morally respectable have not experienced enough forgiveness to be truly moral—if by morality you mean love for others. Thus the morally respectable are not really moral in the best sense of the word. It was this kind of upsetting confrontation which eventually turned the religious establishment against Jesus and resulted in his death on the cross.

Presenting the prophetic meaning. If this parable is to be presented in our day we must be clear that the concrete fact of the immorality of the "morally respectable" is always with us. The task of preserving the meaning of the parable rests with the skill of the interpreter to see this phenomenon and point it out to his congregation.

In order to do what is needed in presenting the irony of moral people who often lose their morality through respectability, it is important not to be entangled in the various levels of logic which seem to be operating in vv. 47–50. The questions of where and in what way the sins of the woman were taken care of, are not issues in the parable. Further, the question of whether Jesus is capable of forgiving sins is not at issue. No, life is not as complex as we make it. All we need to know is that those whom we despise may have an edge on us in love because they have an edge on us in needing and in having found forgiveness.

The humor in this prophetic situation is that our good judgment concerning the logic of the parable always reminds us of the bad judgment of our petty condemnations.

The open-ended nature of this communication is its challenge to explore the terrifying scope of our petty condemnations. The skill we are called to develop is the ability to see this in a concrete and situational way, as opposed to some abstract recognition of the truth.

2. *Parallel 88: The Parable of the Evil Spirit's Return—Matt. 12:43–45/Luke 11:24–26*

Is this a parable? Here we have a borderline case: the form is close to that of a parable, but it also is very close to being a conditional statement. This may simply reflect a traditional Jewish warning about being uncritical about exorcisms.[4] If, on the other hand, it is to be thought of as a parable then the comparison is to the present evil generation, as suggested in Matthew 12:45.

Reconstructing the prophetic situation. This is relatively simple if we conclude that the saying warns against an uncritical acceptance of all exorcisms. Then Jesus is casting doubt on popular notions concerning

4. So Beare, *op. cit.*, pp. 103–4; Bultmann, *op. cit.*, p. 164; Jeremias, *op. cit.*, pp. 197–98.

evil spirits, and asserting that exorcism must be followed by positive action in the life of the one who no longer has the demon.

We may, however, be dealing with something broader than individual exorcism. While I have not seen the suggestion elsewhere, the reference may be to Judaism as a whole. Jesus may be speaking to a people, his people, who are exorcised—that is, monotheistic and morally clean—but otherwise empty. He may be calling for the filling of their religious life, not just the cleansing of it. To be clean is not enough!

It is important in this connection also to note Jeremias's linguistic assertion that the "when" in verses at the beginning of the parable (Matt. 12:43, 44/Luke 11:24, 25) should be replaced by "if." It would then read, "*If* the unclean spirit has gone out of a man, he passes through waterless places. . . . And *if* he comes and finds it empty. . . ."[5]

Presenting the prophetic meaning. The specific application to exorcism is problematic in most Christian settings of our day. But if we have here a word to the people of God that there is more to life than monotheism and morality, then the application to our time becomes clearer. It is common in the church to be more concerned with being "swept clean" than with being filled with new life. This corporate application has great appeal, but is offered here as a clearly tentative interpretation.

5. See Jeremias, *op. cit.,* pp. 197–98.

3. Parallel 90: The Parable of the Sower and/or the Soils—Mark 4:1–9/Matt. 13:1–9/Luke 8:4–8/Thomas 9

Reconstructing the prophetic situation. It is fortunate that this parable comes early in our study. With its concept of parabolic secret, and its supplemental allegorical key (Mark 4:13–20 and parallels) this parable must be credited with having set in motion the theory of interpretation which held sway in the church until the time of Jülicher. We have already pointed this out in our survey of the history of parable interpretation.

If we accept the whole section (Mark 4:1–20 and parallels) as it stands then the prophetic situation is clear. Jesus speaks publicly in parables (to a large crowd beside the sea) but does not really have faith that his own people will truly repent. He therefore intends to confuse them by using the parable form as a type of secret saying. The crowds will think that they see the point, but will in fact be deceived. And because they did not really get the point they will not be capable of turning from their ways and repenting (Mark 4:11–12). Matthew even expands this concept by pointing to this as the fulfillment of Isaiah 6:9–10: Jesus' parables are seen to share in the "hardening" of Israel. The disciples are spared this fate by learning the real message of the parable from Jesus in private.

The position of most modern scholarship since Jülicher has been to call the secrecy motif and the allegorical interpretation into question. The prophetic situation is different. The message of the parable in vv. 2–8 is clear: the story moves through situations of discouragement to one of final satisfaction at the good harvest. Such a dynamic implies that Jesus was holding out a message of hope in the face of definite discouragement. Could it be that Jesus was reflecting on his own ministry and its trials and frustrations? This might be a helpful interpretation, but we need to remember Jeremias's warning about the importance of keeping the eschatological setting in mind. Jesus' message is eschatological: the kingdom of God is at hand. This is a proclamation of hope. The parable announces hope at the final harvest, and the prior difficulties reflect either Jesus' own ministry or the experience of the disciples in following him. Paul speaks of this combination of discouragement and hope in many places (e.g., Rom. 8:31–39). Here we have, then, an important aspect concerning Jesus which we often overlook. He did not just talk about the cross, suffering, and commitment. He also spoke—as in this parable—words of encouragement.

Presenting the prophetic meaning. The greatest difficulty in presenting the meaning of this parable may well be in discovering its contemporary setting. The old allegorical interpretation has persevered with such vigor that many who theoretically reject the allegorical key still retain something of that interpretation—that we be good soils—in their preaching. The sermon comes out something like, "We will have victory, and, by the way, be good listeners (soil) to the word of God."

Modern scholarship says something different. There is a single message: in spite of difficulties there is victory. The proper application of the gospel in this parable is to identify those present day difficulties which might cause the people of God to despair of any hope for progress in the church.

The humor here is that Jesus is a bit more relaxed than the normal high-pressure reformer or revolutionary prophet. He is not just a sectarian prophet of doom, but is rather a man who sees clear difficulties while at the same time holding out hope for himself and his followers. Over and against the "pouting prophetic preacher" Jesus comes across with the humor of patience. Even as he hung on the cross he could ask, "Forgive them for they know not what they do." In our present situation can we see any hope on the other side of the difficulties? If not, have we truly caught the vision of Jesus? The humor of this is that Jesus is able to pull us away from the difficulty of the moment in order to see the broader perspective. When we listen to the simple message of the parable itself, there is a new picture of Jesus which emerges. He is no longer the esoteric teacher engaged in hardening the people of Israel so that they will be judged by God; he is rather the master who calls us all to be of cheer in the midst of difficulties. Here is a word to the church today! To choose this meaning instead of allegory is obviously no academic exercise.

4. Parallel 95: The Parable of the Patient Husbandman—Mark 4:26–29

Reconstructing the prophetic situation. The first question about this parable is whether all the verses originated with Jesus. Bultmann feels that the introductory phrase, "the kingdom of God is like," is not original.[6] Beare contends that v. 29 is secondary, a later effort to buttress the parable with a quotation from Scripture (Joel 3:13).[7] All of these attempts seem based on very little evidence; one can just as well think of vv. 26–29 as a unity.

Taken as a unity, the parable asserts that there is a time for waiting and a time for action. This is true for the farmer, and also in the kingdom of God. The time of waiting is like a man who sleeps and rises, day and night. He does this because the seed grows of itself, or to use the Greek in closer translation, the seed grows automatically (*automatē*). The time of action is the time of harvest where the sickle is put to use.

There is no hint in the text concerning the situation in which this plea for patience was spoken. Many scholars have suggested that this was likely a word of Jesus when there was unrest in his country on account of the Zealots' clamor for an immediate revolt against Roman rule.[8] By this interpretation the parable says, "Forget completely about the method of revolt" or, "Forget about the revolt *now,* perhaps *later* will be the time." The choice between these alternatives depends in part on whether or not v. 29 is accepted as part of the parable. Because I feel that that verse can legiti-

---

6. Bultmann, *op. cit.,* p. 173.

7. Beare, *op. cit.,* p. 114.

8. This suggestion is at least as old as 1903, see C. A. Bugge, *Die Hauptparabeln Jesu* (Giessen, 1903), 1:157 ff. It is also found more recently in Jeremias, *op. cit.,* p. 152, and Beare, *op. cit.,* p. 114.

mately be taken as part of the parable, the message I get is to *wait now,* and *act later* at the proper time, the harvest time.

There are reasons for choosing this interpretation. It fits with Jesus' double-edged statement, "Give to Caesar what is Caesar's, but to God what is God's." Not all obedience to the state is justified, only some—but the limits of propriety are not identified. Jesus was not enough of an outright revolutionary to be a Zealot, but he was a dangerous man or he would not have been crucified, the special death of enemies of the state. And while Jesus was not himself a Zealot, members of his band of followers clearly were.[9]

There is here an element of humor which ought not be overlooked. The parable does not indicate when the time of the harvest will come. Dodd has claimed that Jesus preaches that the time to "put in the sickle" had arrived.[10] This is not an impossible interpretation, but it is also credible to interpret Jesus as desiring his followers to wait. Is Jesus giving his followers a prescription about waiting or acting? It may be that he is not giving them a direct order, but only laying out some possibilities. He may be saying there is a time for revolt, and a time for waiting; to discern the right time is a task for the disciples to work out. They must decide what to do in a given situation. There is surely an open-ended quality to this parable.

9. Cf. S. G. F. Brandon, *Jesus and the Zealots* (Manchester, 1967).
10. C. H. Dodd, *The Parables of the Kingdom,* rev. ed. (New York: Scribner, 1961), p. 179.

A critical reservation is in order. While it may well be that political revolt against Rome is the issue of this parable, we cannot know for certain. We can only suggest the political interpretation as a strong possibility. Jesus seems to have been asked about the timing for revolt against the Romans, and he responds with a characteristically double-edged statement.

Presenting the prophetic meaning. Whatever the original setting of the parables there is good reason to keep our application open-ended. It would be tragic to assume that Jesus was giving an exact prescription— either wait or act. He was, rather, suggesting that there are times for both and it is up to us to understand the time. The presentation of this parable must stake a claim for an open-ended way of looking at the gospel and life in the kingdom of God.

This supports neither quietism or activism, but rather careful discernment of situations and times. If the one who speaks this parable in the name of Jesus has neither the wisdom to wait when necessary, nor the courage to act when proper, then the church is the loser.

5. Parallel 96: The Parable of the Weeds and the Wheat—Matt. 13:24–30/Thomas 57

Reconstructing the prophetic situation. This parable is like the parable of the sower in that an allegorical explanation is given along with it. As is the case with the sower, so here. The explanation of the parable of the weeds and the wheat (vv. 36–43) misses the point of the parable which is in fact a call for patience: wait for the harvest before separating the good from the bad.[11] Jeremias has shown in a most elaborate way that the language of the explanation is that of Matthew and not Jesus. The language also reflects terms which were first used in the setting of the early church, not in the life of Jesus.[12] We see again the same old tendency of some in the early community to add interpretations to the parables which are in the style of allegorical elaborations which miss the real dynamics of the parable itself.

The story turns around the concern of the servants that the weeds be taken out before the time of harvest, but the householder chooses to wait until the harvest to separate the weeds from the wheat. Beare feels that the natural movement of the story is disturbed both by the mention of the enemy who sows weeds in the wheat (v. 25) and by the subsequent discussion of the servants and householder (vv. 27–28a). The parable can indeed read just as well if it merely suggests that there was a planting, that weeds grew up in a natural way along with the wheat, that there was a discussion between the servants and the householder about whether or not to pull the weeds up, and that finally the householder decided to be patient (v. 29).[13] The punch line in any reconstruction of the original parable form has to be the same, that is, v. 29: "No; lest in

11. See Jeremias, *op. cit.*, p. 81, and Bultmann, *op. cit.*, p. 187.
12. See Jeremias, *op. cit.*, pp. 81–85. This extensive presentation of linguistic evidence must be read in detail to be fully appreciated!
13. See Beare, *op. cit.*, p. 117.

gathering the weeds you root up the wheat along with them."

To sum up:

1. Most commentators reject the explanation in vv. 36–43 as secondary and beside the point.

2. Some feel that the mention of the enemy sowing the weeds in the field and the discussion about the enemy in vv. 27–28a is also secondary allegory and beside the point.

3. Some feel that v. 30 is anti-climactic and secondary.

4. The whole of the parable, vv. 24–30, can be accepted as original.

As long as we remember that v. 29 is the main verse in the parable, I see no difficulty in accepting the text of vv. 24–30 as they stand. The dynamics of this point to the problem of the coexistence of the weeds and the wheat and the necessity of not overreacting to the situation. Patience and wisdom are the way to handle the situation.

Most important is the possible situation behind this type of parable. One situation which would fit is the tendency in Judaism of various sects to strive for a pure community. The Pharisees rejected the common people as the "people of the earth." The Essenes rejected mainline Judaism as the establishment of the devil. When Jesus came with a message for publicans and sinners as well as for the religious, he was speaking about the necessity for the good and the bad learning to live together. Jesus thus says that God is the judge, and anyone who wishes now to have a pure community is likely not to purify the community but only to tear it up.

Presenting the prophetic meaning. It must be pointed out how crusades against evil can end up as nonproductive even though the original intention was laudable. The parable is highly situational. Not all intentions to expose evil or purify the community are equally nonproductive, but some are. Jesus clearly felt that the situation he was referring to was of this latter nature. Jesus is condemning not all moralists, but the kind of moralist—surely familiar in our day—who with religious fervor engages in witch hunts and deals in bitter polemics against sin. The picture has an ironic humor, for Jesus laughs at those who limit their morality to an opposition to sin.

6. *Parallel 97: The Parable of the Mustard Seed— Mark 4:30–32/Matt. 13:31–32/Luke 13:18–19/ Thomas 20*

Reconstructing the prophetic situation. It is difficult to reconstruct the situation out of which this parable comes. One possibility is simply that Jesus was speaking to his disciples, telling them not to be discouraged, there was much in store for them in their ministry. Another possibility is that of a debate with the Pharisees or some other group who might have held to an exclusive understanding of the kingdom of God. Then the ending would be an affirmation that the kingdom is big enough to include everyone, even the outcasts. Neither possibility significantly alters the meaning of the parable.

Presenting the prophetic meaning. This parable is more like a pronouncement than a story which suddenly changes direction. I see it as a relatively straightforward message which is not difficult to handle. Jesus' ministry may have had small beginnings (in Galilee) but it will have great effect because it is God's kingdom. The same thought can be seen in the Old Testament (Ezek. 17:32; Dan. 4:21) where the same figure of the tree furnishing the nesting place for the birds is used.

7. Parallel 98: The Parable of the Leaven— Matt. 13:33/Luke 13:20–22/Thomas 96

This parable is most likely a doublet with the parable of the mustard seed. That Matthew and Luke present them together points to their paired existence in the Q source. It may even be that they were spoken by Jesus in a pair.

8. Parallel 101: The Parables of the Treasure and the Pearl—Matt. 13:44–46/Thomas 109 and 76

Reconstructing the prophetic situation. There are several issues which need to be sorted out in this double parable:

1. Were they originally intended to stand together as a double parable?
2. Is the phrase, "all that he has," original or secondary?
3. Is the stress on self-denial, joy, or making the plunge at the proper time?

4. Is the best reading in v. 44 "all that he has," or "what he has"?

5. To whom is the parable spoken?

There is a sharp difference of opinion as to whether these two parables were originally spoken as a double parable.[14] Such a disagreement is impossible to settle and for our purposes takes historical concern too far. From the standpoint of central meaning, the parables make the same point whether they were spoken by Jesus as a pair or not, although Jeremias goes too far in asserting that the meaning of the parables is identical with no distinction between the dynamics of the two.[15] Jeremias thus illustrates how scholastic exegesis of the New Testament at times fails to see that emotional tone is a significant part of meaning. The same thing is being said, but the two stories have slight but significantly different twists to them.

It is also interesting to note how blindness to the difference in emotional coloration also leads these same scholars to ignore the solid facts of different textual evidence for readings in the two parables. In the parable of the pearl the man who buys the pearl sells "all" that he has to make the purchase. There is unanimity in the various textual traditions on this reading. The idea is therefore universally accepted: the seeker of the pearl made a total sale of all his possessions to gain the pearl of value. However, the same does not seem to be the

14. Bultmann, *op. cit.,* p. 173 argues against them being a double parable. Jeremias holds the opposite, claiming that both parables express exactly the same meaning. See Jeremias, *op. cit.,* pp. 200–201.

15. See Jeremias, *op. cit.,* p. 200.

case with the parable of the treasure in the field. Here we find disagreement in the textual traditions. Some texts read that the man sold "all" he had for the purchase of the field, and other texts read that he sold possessions (not necessarily all of them) and bought the field. I would hold that this later way of putting it is the original text, and to be preferred.[16] With or without this textual argument it is clear that the purchase of a field with a hidden value is different from the purchase of a pearl of known value.

This brings us to the question of the intent of the parables. Modern interpreters are correct in criticizing any attempt to make self-denial the chief message of the parables. With respect to the parable of the hidden treasure we would even go one step beyond some modern interpretations. In that parable it is especially important to note that the story has an element of intrigue in it. If one attempts to show that such action is legal, the humor in the story is missed.[17] The man finds and covers up the hidden treasure, and the parable invites us to imagine how he sells some property in order to get money to buy the land. Though there is nothing said, we can well imagine the man acting casual about buying the land so as not to arouse suspicion. We can then reflect on double joy: first of discovering the

16. Of the modern editions of the New Testament, the Nestle text supports the above judgment, Codex Vaticanus supplying the major evidence. It appears that the attempt to make the language in the two parables parallel accounts for the tradition which states that the man purchasing the field sold "all" just like the man buying the pearl.

17. Jeremias admits the question of morality is not at stake, but he has to go on and prove that the action of the man in buying the field with the hidden treasure is legal. He misses the humor. Jeremias, *op. cit.*, p. 199.

hidden treasure, and then actually possessing it without having to pay full value for it. What is being said? I take the point to be one of satisfaction. The man who has "bought in" on the good news knows the value of what he has, even if others do not. In fact, at the moment of sale only he knows the true value of what is being purchased.

The parable of the pearl has a slightly different twist, though the same general point is being made. The man comes across the valuable pearl, but in this case the value is apparently known to both buyer and seller. To make the purchase our man must go out and sell all he has to buy the pearl. The seller is out to get all he can from the sale. The element of giving up in order to get what you want is more in the foreground. As Linnemann has pointed out, "There is a basic difference between a purchase price and a sacrifice."[18]

The point of the parables seems to center around a stress on the value which can be found in the kingdom of God. You may simply stumble on this value, or may find it after a long search. No matter, once you find it you buy it with speed. It does not really matter whether you get it for a bargain or have to sell everything you have. What does matter is that you purchase it.

We may now ask about the original audience. Matthew gives no help, but we can discern something from the fact that the message is one in which timing and risk were of importance. It seems sensible to suppose that this parable was aimed at the disciples in a

18. See Eta Linnemann, *Jesus of the Parables* (New York: Harper & Row, 1966), p. 100. Purchase is giving for value received. Sacrifice is giving without thought of return.

moment of decision. We have no way of knowing what that moment of decision might have been, but Jesus is saying that at such moments the lessons we learn in business life about buying and selling are of great importance. The mood of a follower of Jesus must at times parallel that of the buyer who has found what he wants and acts quickly to get it. Such risk brings great satisfaction. Jesus may not have been calling for the great once-and-for-all sacrifice; he may rather have been calling his disciples to a particular set of decisive actions. Whatever it was, Jesus was pointing to the joy of possessing something of value after the risk was taken. Religion is more than being good, it is also action —to get that which is of value.

Presenting the prophetic meaning. Here is no heavy-handed message. The image of life which comes in this parable is one of imagination, verve, bold practicality, and joy. This is not the parable for the religious pessimist. We risk and even pay to live truly, but the treasure *is* true life! The parable does not *compel* belief in the gospel. Rather, it presents the gospel as something worth having. May it not still be worth noting that the church all too often stresses price rather than value?

9. Parallel 102: The Parable of the Net— Matt. 13:47–48

Reconstructing the prophetic situation. This parable has received radically different treatments in modern scholarship. There is general agreement about the sec-

ondary character of vv. 49–50 because of the added
detailed imagery which suggests allegory and also limits
the meaning of the parable to the last judgment. The
difference of opinion occurs around the meaning of the
two remaining verses, 47 and 48.

Beare and Manson reject the reference to the sorting
out of the fish (v. 48) as also being secondary. To them
the one verse parable (v. 47) refers to the inclusiveness
of the kingdom of God in the proclamation of Jesus.
The kingdom calls to everyone. The addition of judgment is seen as the stress of Matthew, a stress which
also alters the familiar parable of the great banquet.[19]
This is an appealing argument stressing that Jesus' call
is to all men, and that Matthew has altered it to be an
appeal only to the good.

Dodd accepts the originality of v. 48 and interprets
it to refer to the judgment in history, not the judgment
at the end of the age. He sees Jesus calling all men, but
also confronting them with the demand of the gospel so
that there is a sifting process which always goes on.[20]
This is also an interpretation which has a great deal of
appeal, and seems consistent with other sayings of Jesus
in the Gospels.

Jeremias also accepts the originality of v. 48 but interprets it as referring to the final judgment at the close
of history. He sees this parable as having the same
meaning as that of the weeds among the wheat.[21]

---

19. See Beare, *op. cit.,* p. 119, and T. W. Manson, *The Sayings of Jesus* (London: S.C.M., 1949), p. 197 (as cited in Beare).
20. Dodd, *op. cit.,* pp. 151–52.
21. Jeremias, *op. cit.,* pp. 224–26.

I can find no linguistic or historical-critical evidence to allow a choice of one reconstruction of this parable as being objectively better than any other. Perhaps one can take the easy way out and combine the best of all the interpretations. Was Jesus trying to stress both the inclusiveness of the kingdom and also the process of sifting and judgment in history and at the end of history? That is perhaps the best tentative solution. It is not clear whether the category of the prophetic throws any special light on this passage. We will leave this parable with these moderating comments and allow the reader to judge for himself.

10. Parallel 136: The Parable of the Unmerciful Servant—Matt. 18:23–35

Reconstructing the prophetic situation. Again we must ask whether a specific or a general interpretation of a parable is most helpful. Generally, this story says that men ought to be forgiving toward each other on account of the great forgiveness of God.[22] Jeremias, however, brings out an eschatological meaning by referring this parable to the last judgment. Jesus is seen as warning his people of the judgment of God which is to come at the end of the age. If the people have been a forgiving people they will also be forgiven by God. If not, they will be judged.[23]

Certainly Jesus wished to point out that man's forgiveness of man is prompted by God's boundless mercy. Mercy produces mercy. However, did Jesus wish to

22. So Beare, *op. cit.,* p. 152.
23. Jeremias, *op. cit.,* p. 214.

make only a general point? It would seem that behind the general principle that forgiveness is to be given, is an implicit criticism of forgiveness which was being withheld. Jesus may in fact have told this parable in a situation of injustice in order to reveal what was going on. In a situational way Jesus was saying more than, "Be for forgiveness." He was perhaps pointing toward a specific instance in which his people, or a group of his people, were in fact unforgiving in a minor matter even though they had been shown great mercy. If we remember that most of his preaching was intensely concrete and situational by nature, then the ironic edge comes out. "Is it not tragic that those who have received mercy can in this case refuse to be merciful?"

Presenting the prophetic meaning. The proclamation of this parable need not stop with the abstract call to mercy or the future possibility of judgment. Are there specific instances where we have shown little mercy in contrast to the great mercy shown us? To translate this parable demands more than sensitivity to the language of Jesus. It also demands sensitivity to the situation in which we find ourselves. In order for this parable to come alive in our day there is need for prophets who have vision to see the incongruity in life and speak out about it. That requires humor, humility, and courage.

11. Parallel 144: The Parable of the Good Samaritan—Luke 10:25–37

Reconstructing the prophetic situation. The parable now under consideration has a generalizing introduction ("And who is my neighbor?") which is often taken to be the subject of the parable. Unfortunately the dynamics of the parable would have to be changed to accommodate to such a question. Then the parable would have a man walking down the road to Jerusalem and finding both a fellow countryman and a foreigner robbed and beaten. Then the man must ask the question about the identity of the neighbor and conclude that the foreigner is also the neighbor. While it is commonly recognized that the introductory question is not the whole of the story, most scholars have found it difficult to escape the temptation to moralize the parable. This is true even of those who are committed to remove moralization as secondary to the parables.[24]

We have to ask whether the prophetic interpretation sheds light on the situation. We see the contrast to be between three men. They are not objects of love, but agents of love. Two act by ignoring the situation, while one responds in love to the situation. The parable then also relates what the Samaritan does in caring for the victim of the robbery. The question to ask is how the people who first heard that story might have reacted. Is the important item the precise manner in which the Samaritan went about his act of mercy? Such is not the case. Anyone in Jesus' hearing would likely recognize the Samaritan's action as a standard kind of compassionate acting. What was somewhat unusual is the favorable attitude deliberately shown to the foreigner. In that light Jesus is saying, "Look my friends, this foreigner is doing better by his action than we."

24. So Beare, *op. cit.*, p. 160: "The true spirit of love does not seek to classify and delimit the objects of its compassion, but pours itself out on anyone who is in need." Also Jeremias, *op. cit.*, p. 205: "No human being was beyond the range of his charity."

Jesus is thus not trying to describe what love is, but to activate his people to loving action. He uses a form of irony, saying in effect, "If you want to be a true member of the people of God, do as this foreigner did." There is, as is well known, a tradition of Samaritan stories with this motive in the Gospels. In the healing of the ten lepers the thankful one was a Samaritan, and Jesus asks why only the foreigner is thankful (Luke 17:11–19). The woman at the well in John 4 is Samaritan. These stories place the Samaritan in a role similar to that of the outcast in the ministry of Jesus. It is important in this connection to note that the outcast is not always the object of pity. He is also the example of faith. This latter outlook is what accounts for the presence of the Samaritan in the parable. He is the man of faith, not the object of love.

The prophetic message in this parable is a call to the people of God at least to come to the level of virtue found in the outside world. The parable is an offensive statement. It is important to note that the opening question of 29 is not answered. The parable does not teach who my neighbor is, but asks me to contemplate the unpleasant fact that those who are outside my circle and religion might be better persons than I. They are, indeed, my examples. This leaves us with an open-ended situation. Anyone who proves to be a worthy example is worth looking toward, even though he is not faithful to my religion only.

We miss the point of the story by thinking it to be a condemnation of Judaism in particular. It is a condemnation of smugness. The dynamics of the postparable conversation between the lawyer and Jesus make it clear

81

that the lawyer is capable of making the right judgment and he does receive Jesus' charge to go and do as the Samaritan did. Thus the story is incisive without being sarcastic; it allows the listener to move forward.

The context of the parable in the ministry of Jesus must clearly have been a debate concerning the exclusiveness of Judaism. Were the people of the establishment capable of seeing themselves in the parable? We have a question and answer situation like that of 2 Samuel. The lawyer comes through with the correct answer to Jesus' crucial question. To ask who is a neighbor, and to prove yourself to be a neighbor are two different things. It is possible that the introductory question was not asked in the original situation, but added by later tradition. However, it is perhaps better to see the opening question, v. 29, as original and then observe that Jesus does not directly respond to that question. The method of the parable is to restate questions so that new perspectives for life appear.

Presenting the prophetic meaning. The easy way of presenting this parable is to say that we ought to love the man on the road, the victim of the robbery. But this is only half the message. It is equally important for us to see that the man who acts is a foreigner. White Americans would do well to present this as the parable of the good Jew or the merciful black man. The priest and the Levite are not outside our circle, they belong to our group which passes by while the man who stops to give aid (the Samaritan) is part of another group. In today's world mercy is shown by men and women who are not Christian. By pointing to them we do what

Christ did when he pointed to the good Samaritan. We do this, not out of sarcasm, but in order to raise the vision of fellow believers.

12. Parallel 147: The Parable of the Friend at Midnight—Luke 11:5–8

Reconstructing the prophetic situation. It is encouraging to note that on this parable there is one commentator who is willing to see the vivid and humorous elements.[25] The scene is humorous indeed. A man attempts to raise his neighbor out of bed at midnight because he needs to borrow three loaves of bread to feed a friend who has just arrived from a journey. In situations like that you ask the neighbor, even if he grumbles, because there is nothing else to do. And you know that the neighbor will come to the door with the bread even if he is sleepy and grumpy. The implication seems to be that if you can ask from a friend even at a bad time, you can ask of God at all times.[26]

We have no way of knowing whether there was some specific situation behind this parable, a debate perhaps about the propriety of praying to God for a specific item. It would seem likely that there may well have been such a discussion, possibly covering the general subject of prayer.

Presenting the prophetic meaning. Assuming that the parable did not arise out of a general discussion on prayer, but was a comment arising out of a specific

25. Beare, *op. cit.,* p. 162.
26. So Jeremias, *op. cit.,* p. 159, and Beare, *op. cit.,* p. 162.

situation, it might be best in the presentation of this parable to deal with the fact that many think that in certain situations prayer to God is not proper. We ought to be as willing to approach God for things as we are to approach our neighbor; he will respond as well or better than our neighbor. In point of fact our requests of God suggest that we do not feel as secure with him as we do with friends.

Most important, we must recognize the one simple point this parable makes and avoid undue expansion.

13. Parallel 156: The Parable of the Rich Fool— Luke 12:16–21/Thomas 63

Reconstructing the prophetic situation. It is important to note immediately that vv. 13–14 about covetousness, and v. 21 about laying up treasures for God, are not part of the parable. Beare holds this parable to be a popular tale not originally spoken by Jesus.[27] Jeremias thinks of this as a pronouncement that the end of the age is at hand.[28] The setting is the end of the age *or* the end of the life of a man.

Beyond the historical question it should be pointed out that there is little which our prophetic understanding can say in clarification of the parable. The parable is neither particularly humorous or open-ended. It is a pronouncement of the nearness of the end and the necessity for all to be watchful.

27. Beare, *op. cit.,* p. 168.
28. Jeremias, *op. cit.,* p. 165.

14. Parallel 162: The Parable of the Barren Fig Tree—Luke 13:6–9

Reconstructing the prophetic situation. Jeremias has pointed to the commonness of this story of bearing fruit. The imagery easily lends itself to religious use. There is an important and interesting feature which Jeremias observes in this story: the pleading of the vine-dresser for an additional year of grace before the barren tree is cut down. Is the figure of the gardener used to point to Jesus himself? This possibility may be worth following insofar as Jesus is seen as a prophet who not only calls his people to repentance, but also pleads with God on their behalf.[29]

Beare has offered an important warning, not to take the Lucan context as the key to the meaning, for the context in Luke is the call for repentance, while this parable actually deals with the delay in judgment caused by the mercy of the gardener and the owner of the vineyard.

A final question is whether this parable is addressed to a person or a group. Most would say this parable is addressed to the people as a whole with the message that there is still time to repent and bear fruit.

Presenting the prophetic meaning. Since in our day the image of the prophet is one of sternness and anger, it is well to stress the mercy and kindness of the prophet both in the history of the movement and also in Jesus himself. Otherwise the aspect of kindness may be

29. Jeremias, *op. cit.,* p. 170.

glossed over when only the final lines of the story are seen.

15. Parallel 169: The Parable of the Choice Places at the Banquet—Luke 14:7–11 (also found in Matt. 20:28 in some ancient texts)

Reconstructing the prophetic situation. We have a difficult question when we approach this parable and its setting. V. 7 suggests that the parable was uttered at a banquet in the face of improper conduct on the part of the guests. The context in Luke shows that a whole series of sayings are introduced in this same banquet setting. We may therefore suspect the grouping to be more Lucan than historical. If this is a parable worthy of consideration it may involve more than Jesus' comments concerning the table manners of his fellow countrymen.[30]

I would suppose the situation to be the state of the religious establishment of the day. Jesus is saying that there is a similarity between the quest for honor in the religious establishment and the same quest in a banquet. He outlines the best steps for securing the place of honor. One has to act cool and collected and seek out the low place first. This is certainly not a surefire method, but Jesus says that the host *may* come and see you and elevate you to the place of honor. Then won't

30. Jeremias limits the parable to the banquet setting and calls it a comment on the table manners of the time. *Op. cit.,* p. 192. The banquet setting is seen as secondary by Beare, *op. cit.,* p. 169, and Bultmann, *op. cit.,* pp. 334–36.

that be a feather in your cap! The parable may well end without the generalizing comment in v. 11.

It is important to see that this parable is to be read with a sense of humor. It is a spoof on the religious establishment—comparable to recent advice on how to become a bishop without being religious. If we were to take Jesus without such humor we would have to conclude that he is advocating a type of deceptive maneuvering. This would surely be a forced interpretation.

The setting for the parable is a time when the religious leaders and folk within the synagogues spent a good part of their energy rising to places of honor in the congregation or hierarchy. By suggesting a better way, Jesus is only making fun of the whole process.

Presenting the prophetic meaning. It is important for us to be able to laugh at the way we maneuver for power, and to help others to the same perspective. Not that we should seriously pursue humility after piously rejecting pride, that would only increase the pride present in the humorless quest to be the *most* humble person around. We need to see Jesus smiling at his followers as he spoke this parable. Just relax, there is room for all in the kingdom.

16. Parallel 171: The Parable of the Tower Builder and the King Contemplating a Campaign—Luke 14:28–32

Reconstructing the prophetic situation. It is important to note the general context of these twin parables.

They are set between two sayings on self-denial (Luke 14:25–27 and Luke 14:33), although as many have pointed out there is a difference between prudent self-examination and self-denial.[31] We must here pause for a moment and allow the realism and calculation of Jesus' words to sink in. How could the same Christ who called us to take up our cross and follow him also counsel us to this type of deliberate calculation? One solution would be to conclude that one type of advice comes from Jesus and the other from the early church. I do not, however, find that a helpful solution.

My suggestion is to see that the scope of discipleship on some occasions demands self-denial, and on other occasions calls for a prudent calculation. This may indeed give a fuller picture of what it means to follow Christ. We can see many errors in the history of the church when the church failed first to sit down to count the cost. We are not given any hint in the parable as to the precise occasion for this advice, but the advice itself is clear. Building a tower or waging a war can be too costly. Translated into the religious situation, certain activities can also be too costly. Before we set out on some tasks or engage in some battles there ought to be a cost accounting. The sacrifice in life, money, effort, or pain may not be worth it. Better put, we have only so much energy at our disposal.

As a counterbalance to the advice of Jesus about spending ourselves without counting the cost, we en-

---

31. Against this point of view is Beare, *op. cit.,* p. 177. Supporting such a view is Jeremias, *op. cit.,* p. 112, n. 91; also Bultmann, *op. cit.,* p. 171.

counter this advice to first count the cost. It may be that Luke has combined these different statements in order for the reader to do his own balancing. It is now up to the individual Christian and the particular congregation to figure out which situation calls for maximum sacrifice and which calls for calculation.

Presenting the prophetic meaning. We can only offer some hints along the way about the invocation of these two parables in the service of the gospel. If the crisis calls for total commitment, then it may be that the ministry, in the long perspective, requires the kind of cost accounting seen in tower building and battle plans. If a congregation decides to take on a long-range project, it is necessary to look to the cost. Many items may be worth doing, but there are only limited resources. Similarly, individuals may also wish to perform certain tasks for the kingdom, but may be lacking in the necessary emotional or intellectual strength. One man's tower may be another man's ruin. One man's victory may be another man's defeat. Paul said that we have differing gifts, and this calls for calculation when particular tasks are faced. The one who calls for such calculation is not likely to be called a prophet. However, having programs falter halfway to the grand objective, or working to the point of nervous breakdown is not necessarily doing our best for the kingdom. Being prophet and minister does not mean being unrealistic, but rather doing things for God in the right season. These two parables suggest that work for the kingdom is aimed at the final score, not at the grandstand.

17. *Parallel 172: The Parables of the Lost Sheep and the Lost Coin—Luke 15:1–10*

Luke 15. If the parable of the sower in Mark 4 is the pole from which the allegorical interpretation of the parables received its impetus, then Luke 15 is the anchor for the modern versions of that theory. The introductory verses in the chapter point to the parables as public utterances of Jesus used in this case in the framework of his debate with the Pharisees and scribes. They also stand with little or no interpretive material added, thus underlining the parable as an open and pointed statement.

Luke 15 is also important as a demonstration of how we might go beyond that historical criticism which simply limits these parables to one simple thrust. Literary analysis reminds us of the complexity of picture story communication. In one sense all three parables say the same thing, namely, God loves sinners. Communication in a picture story is always more than the presentation of an idea; it is an idea supported by an emotional and situational impact. While all three stories may indeed be saying the same thing about God's love for sinners, there are non-verbal impressions which come from the story itself which must be taken into account. Put in another way, there is the denotation or the main point, but also there is the connotation given by the story form. An ordinary sentence carries a connotative meaning, but the parable as a story form carries connotation to a higher degree. Thus it is that there may be one major theme in Luke 15, but there are also variations on that theme. When this is seen the variations in the argument of Jesus with his opponents become evident. It is all too easy to think of a stereotyped argument between Jesus and the Pharisees. This chapter, however, requires us to do more.

Reconstructing the prophetic situation in the parable of the lost sheep. There is general agreement that Luke rather than Matthew offers the correct historical setting for the parable of the lost sheep. Luke tells the story in response to the questioning of the scribes and the Pharisees about why Jesus would consider eating with sinners. This is a more believable context than Matthew's which sets the parable in the ecclesiastical setting of Jesus' conversation with his disciples in which he uses the parable to assert that the insignificant in the church are not to be lost.[32] (There is no reason, however, for refusing to extend this parable to concern for the insignificant.)

It may be that the parable was originally spoken as a twin to the parable of the lost coin, as Luke has it. Scholars have observed that Luke may have possessed a special source of parables from which he draws those that appear in chapter 15.[33]

It is generally accepted that the main thought in the parable is joy over finding the lost. This joy is highlighted by a contrast between the situation in which the shepherd discovers the loss, and the moment when the sheep is found. What I should like to stress is the

---

32. See Linnemann, *op. cit.,* p. 43; also Jeremias, *op. cit.,* p. 132.
33. See Beare, *op. cit.,* pp. 177–78.

threatening statement that the shepherd left the ninety-nine sheep in the hill country and set off on the search. Jeremias tries to point out that no good oriental shepherd would leave the ninety-nine alone. This may be, but the parable makes just that point.[34] Thus if the shepherd leaves his flock to fare for itself in the hill country, it is a threat which is being directed to the Pharisees and scribes. Jesus is saying that a shepherd can, at the loss of one of the little sheep, do a foolish thing and leave the rest exposed to danger because of his high emotional reaction to the pain in his loss of the one.

If we are correct about the setting, then the parable is in response not to a criticism of God, but of Jesus. The Pharisees would be saying to him, as it were: "Look here. The people in this country who have lapsed from the synagogue worship are lost and it is not worth the effort to spend so much time with them. Furthermore, you should realize that in being so concerned with the rejects of our society you are giving the impression that you do not care about the righteous." This parable is a response in harsh words. A shepherd can do extreme things in his grief. He does not sit down and deliberately think about leaving the ninety-nine, but he might just do it anyway. Jesus is thus saying that his action may well have an element of risk in it. Still he acts out of his concern for the lost in the house of Israel. When you set out on a rescue mission you do not calculate the cost. There is an abandon, a moment of

34. This is a case where the scholarship needs a little humor. Jesus may have his characters do foolish things once in a while. See Jeremias, *op. cit.*, pp. 133–34.

intense emotion, in the search for the lost. It is not true to the logic of economics at all points, but it is true to the logic of love.

Presenting the prophetic meaning. The wise man and the prophet do not always agree. The wise man has to look at the whole situation. He has to balance the time and the effort needed to find the lost one against the danger in leaving ninety-nine sheep in the wilderness. The prophet might not always do this. There is an element of insensitivity in his action.

How is it with the church? Is the church always to think of the total situation, or is it willing at times to be swept away for a time to a burning issue? There is a sarcastic note in the momentary desertion of the righteous. Could we for a moment leave the comfort of the congregation and its walls and venture into the street? Jesus is not saying that at every moment of its life the church is to forget the righteous and live dangerously, but there are times. The preacher has the task of showing his people that a risk for the lost is sometimes very necessary, even if the chairman of the church council is offended.

Jeremias has also pointed out an interesting contrast in the way this story is recorded in the Gospel of Thomas. In that account the sheep which is lost is the biggest in the flock. What the tradition found in Thomas failed to note was the paradoxical nature of the love of Jesus for the lost or the least. Such a presentation robs the illustration of its description of the radical nature of God's grace and Jesus' ministry.[35]

35. See Jeremias, *op. cit.,* p. 133.

Reconstructing the prophetic situation in the parable of the lost coin. Here the emotional thrust of the parable is different, although otherwise the point is the same. The woman is upset about the loss of the coin, and happy when she finds it. Abandoning the other coins is not considered. The search operation is not pictured as a dangerous operation, but rather as a diligent one. We all know the difference between looking for a lost person or an animal and searching for a coin or other object. In looking for a lost sheep there is the feeling of haste so as to prevent the animal from dying or being harmed. When the search is for a coin in a house there is the frustration of having lost it, but no sense of haste because the coin will not run away. There is justification for some laughter at the figure of the housewife fretting about the coin.

This difference of emotional impact implies a subtle shift of meaning in the context. With the lost coin there is no implication the established church will be neglected in the search for the lost. Here there is no equivalent to the implied threat that the ninety-nine sheep were left in the hill country alone. The change of pace in the second illustration results in greater stress on what is common to both parallels: a lost coin, or person, is still something of value. Sinners are also of value.

Some scholars have argued that the two concluding statements (Luke 15:7, 10) are additions to the parables. These verses introduce the thought of penitence which is really secondary to the emphasis on the search by the shepherd and the woman.[36] The argument pos-

36. So Beare, *op. cit.,* p. 178.

sesses its point, but not so convincingly as to cause us to reject these verses as words of Jesus. It is certain that the main point of the stories is the search, not the penance. However, Jesus could easily have added the latter without altering the meaning of the parable. If vv. 7 and 10 were spoken by him they add an element of irony to the stories. Jesus would thus be saying that the Pharisees and scribes "think" they do not need to repent, but really they do. Such an ending adds a bite to the story.

Presenting the prophetic meaning. It would be well to note the slightly more humorous setting of the parable of the lost coin in contrast to the story of the lost sheep. Further, this parable includes a penetrating criticism of the righteous in any society who devalue those in their society who have been "lost." Isn't it strange that in the world of finance there is more concern to win back what has been lost, than there is in the religious world? In religion it is all too easy to let the lost be lost.

18. Parallel 173: The Parable of the Elder Brother —Luke 15:11–32

Reconstructing the prophetic situation. Most students and preachers are aware of the discussion as to whether this parable is about the prodigal son or the elder brother. Another common issue is the moralizing trend in most interpretations, a trend which wants to compare the attitude of the elder brother to the prodigal. Of course the prodigal comes off as the better of the two for having repented and accepted God's love. This is of course part of the interpretation, but there is an important aspect of the action in the story which is almost always overlooked. I am referring to the final two verses, 31 and 32, which can be taken as the climax of the story.

In these verses the father comes out to the field and finds the elder brother angry because of the reception for his younger brother. This is rather to be expected. What is unusual and overlooked by most, if not all, interpretations is the kindness of these final two verses. The father does not scold the son as we might expect; he rather assures his older son that they will always be together, and that all the father's estate belongs to the elder brother. It is important to notice this in the dynamics of the story. The father is saying that it is fitting to have a feast of welcome for the return of the prodigal, but that the rights of the elder son will always be respected. The division of the estate which occurred at the beginning of the parable will be honored and the elder son will continue to retain the estate with full rights in the inheritance.

If this is translated into the situation of Jesus' debate with the establishment of his day, a debate about his ministry to the poor, some new angles come to light. Jesus had of course been accused of being revolutionary, and the kind response at the end of this parable would stand in contrast to the harshness of the parable of the lost sheep. The intent in this parable is both to confront and to assure the Pharisee and the rest of the religious establishment. The ministry of Jesus to the poor is not a rejection of the righteous in favor of the sinner. Jesus does wish to reform the religious structures of his day so that they become open to the sinner who repents, but he does not wish to destroy those structures. In the dynamics of the parable the father does not reject the elder son when he accepts the prodigal back. The final line asserts that it is not an either/or with Jesus' ministry. To be for the sinner and his return is only to challenge the jealousy of the righteous. The final goal in the ministry of Jesus is to have the righteous and the sinner accept each other because God accepts them both.

Presenting the prophetic meaning. What is needed here is to understand that Jesus could change his pace in his debate with the religious authorities of his time. Each of the parables in Luke 15 is directed to the same issue, but with differing connotations. Only if the preacher can understand that there are differing aspects to the fight of the believer for the renewal of religion in his day can he begin to see the full scope of meaning in the three parables of this chapter. They need not be considered simultaneously. There are times when the religious establishment needs the hard word, and times when it needs the reassurance that renewal is affirmative in respect to its final goals.

A concern for the lost in society will, of course, confront those who are not concerned. It will also aim at controlling an "elder brother" attitude in the religious community, but this control is not designed to destroy the elder brother but to save him from his own jealousy. In the end this is not just a word for the elder brother alone, it is also a word for those who, in the name of the mercy which Jesus shows to the sinner, condemn the man who is smug. Smugness is also forgivable. In this parable we see smugness confronted and forgiven by a father who loves all his children.

19. Parallel 174: The Parable of the Unjust Stewards—Luke 16:1–7

Reconstructing the prophetic situation. We have limited this parable to its story. Vv. 8–13 must be considered separate sayings. It is possible to consider v. 8 as a proper interpretation of the parable, but it seems unnecessarily forced to have one of the characters in the parable step forward with the interpretation. Jeremias has suggested that this parable was spoken when the hour of decision was at hand for the people Jesus was addressing. Jesus was suggesting quick and resolute action in the face of the judgment which was impending.[37]

If we wish to include v. 8a in the parable, then it is also possible to give it the meaning, "The Lord (Jesus) commended the dishonest steward for his prudence." This leaves us with a very short conclusion but does give direction to the interpretation.[38] Further, it points to the quickness of the steward and asks if the people of God are able to act in such a forthright manner in times of crisis. It is likely that Jesus was pointing to a special situation in his day, but we are not in a position definitely to know what this might be.

37. Jeremias, *op. cit.,* p. 182.
38. See ibid., p. 47 for a fuller discussion of this interpretation of v. 8a.

Beyond this there is darkness about this parable. It is also possible that the real ending of the story is missing and we can only guess at what followed. This parable leaves the reader and preacher with a basic problem which he alone must solve; whether there is enough clarity here to teach anything on the basis of the text as we have it. Actually, only Jeremias has made progress in understanding the story. Our interpretation is tentatively based on his insights.

Presenting the prophetic meaning. Jeremias is clear about the crisis nature of this parable. To act quickly in the face of certain situations in history and life is the highest sign of prudence. To clarify this, it is necessary for any modern exposition to point out what kind of crisis in our day is so grave as to call for such action. Thus the interpreter of the parable must be as versed in the issues of our day as he is in the structure of the text.

20. Parallel 177: The Parable of the Rich Man and Lazarus—Luke 16:19–31

Reconstructing the prophetic situation. Some interpreters see this as a double-edged parable, the first point being the reversal of fortunes, the second being the concluding statement that the brothers would not be convinced if some one were to come from the dead and speak to them. If this analysis is true then there would be some difficulty settling on what is the purpose of the parable in its original setting.[39]

39. Jeremias, *op. cit.,* p. 186.

If we approach this parable in terms of the prophetic situation the conclusion that there are two points to the parable is not very helpful. Working from the general analysis of style we further hold that the ending of a parable most generally reveals what the real point of the plot is, and therefore serves as the best clue to the setting of the parable and its occasion. The final conclusion of this story is that Abraham speaks to the issue of Lazarus being raised from the dead and returning to speak to the brothers of the rich man. The purpose of this journey from the dead is to warn the brothers of the fate of the rich man. The reply of Abraham is full of irony. If the rich man's brothers wished to repent of their ways they have enough at their disposal for that purpose. They have Moses and the prophets, that is, the Old Testament. Abraham reminds the rich man that his brothers can read the words of the Old Testament, and if that would not bring them to repentance, then neither would the sight of a man coming from the dead. Apparently Abraham is delivering out the judgment of Jesus on his situation. The rich in his day seem to be out of touch with truth because they are basically indifferent to God's truth and the suffering of the poor which exists around them. Indifference seems to be the key issue in the closing statement of Abraham.

This would point to a situation of indifference in the ministry of Jesus. What that might be in detail we cannot know. It does appear that Jesus saw the upper classes in his day as shut off from human suffering, and from the truth of God in the Scripture. The real issue does not seem to be the question of inequality alone, but inequality coupled with lack of interest in finding truth. The parable wants to state with emphasis that there is no way to break through the indifference of man with any special tricks like the dead coming back with messages. We seem to have a situation in which Jesus confronted massive indifference and apathy. This story is his response to it. In view of the fact that the brothers of the rich man are written off, the setting in life may be a discussion with his disciples about how to reach the upper class with all its style and sophistication. The disciples may have been thinking of new and more dramatic ways to get the message across, but Jesus' parable comes with the thrust of caution. He is saying that little can be done to communicate with this decadent upper class if they are not open to ordinary communication in the first place. Jesus' point is that the breakdown in communication is due to the unwillingness of the rich to hear.

Presenting the prophetic meaning. It is important in observing the flow of the story to see that no mention is made of the evil of the rich man. He seems to be as respectable as any man in the upper class of his day. Lazarus, the beggar, is given a place to beg by his gate —in that time an act of charity. The crumbs from the table are given to Lazarus. The two men are set side by side in life, yet they have nothing more than that in common. The irony of the story is that only in death does the rich man see any value in Lazarus. Then it is too late, for the gulf of indifference which stands between these two men in life remains for all eternity.

It is significant that the message which the poor man can deliver is akin to the message of Scripture itself. There is a parallel to the wisdom of the poor and the wisdom of Scripture: Jesus' message is good news for the poor. This is a way of looking at wisdom which contrasts with the view that wisdom comes only from study. Jesus' point is to link wisdom with the truth of life. To be sensitive to the cry of suffering is to be wise, a message learned first from the Old Testament prophets.

This parable does not call us to pity Lazarus; he is, rather, a source of wisdom much like the wisdom in Scripture. The mercy of God inclines to the weak, the widow, and the hopeless.

21. Parallel 185: The Parable of the Unjust Judge —Luke 18:1–8

Reconstructing the prophetic situation. It has been often asserted that this parable is not original with Jesus, but comes rather from the early church. The reasons for this view center in an interpretation of vv. 6–8 as secondary—the term, "God's elect," points to the early church in times of persecution waiting for the return of Jesus as the Son of man.[40] These arguments are not the most convincing. The expressions do fit the situation of the early church under persecution, but there is no reason to suspect that this is more than a correct application. Is it not also reasonable to assume that there were difficulties with individuals during the ministry of Jesus which could easily have called forth this parable? The issue is one of discouragement in the

40. See Linnemann, *op. cit.,* p. 121, n. 14, for an extensive summary of the debate.

face of some situation where the difficulties are not being resolved. On the national level this could have had to do with the Roman occupation. Whatever the situation there appears to be hopelessness. God has not answered the prayers of those who cry for help, so what is the purpose of faith? To this situation Jesus responds with this brief parable. It is not one of the greatest of his parables but it does have considerable attraction.

First off, Jesus does not attempt to correct the image of God which often develops in a situation of discouragement. He sets that aside as an unnecessary intellectual debate. The argument grants the fact of injustice. However, we are wiser in our dealings with men than we are in our dealings with God. We continue to deal with a judge whom we may regard as unjust, and we can even have success in the effort. Why not continue in prayer with God? This is a parable of confrontation, but there is an affirmative and open element in the communication of the issue. Whoever is being confronted is not condemned for hopelessness or for any careless statements about God made in that situation. The parable meets discouragement where it is, and tries to help with a word which does not condemn.

Presenting the prophetic meaning. The important issue is not difficult to come to. Jesus is interested in how we handle the situation, not in any incorrect ideas we may or may not have about God. The temptation may be to give long explanations about how it is that Jesus does not really feel that God is unjust, and miss the important point: he did not condemn impious thoughts about God, but rather came to the aid of people in need of encouragement. This same dynamic is echoed in a more profound way in the cry of loneliness made by Jesus himself on the cross. It sounds impious to liken God to an unjust judge, but seen in context, the proclamation of Jesus enters the arena of man's discouragement, not to condemn but to encourage.

22. Parallel 186: The Parable of the Pharisee and the Tax Collector—Luke 18:9–14

Reconstructing the prophetic situation. There is good likelihood that the setting of this parable is accurate. The major problems are the stress on humility in v. 14 and the fact that the story has been told too many times.

T. W. Manson has called the special Lucan section of parables in chapters 15 and 16, "The Gospel of the Outcast." The tradition has preserved for us the valuable information about the setting. Jesus was criticizing the pride of the Pharisees and the force of his critique is clear if we attempt to consider how the prayer of the Pharisee may have sounded to those who heard the parable for the first time. It is difficult for us to imagine this since we know so well how the story turns out. From a technical and theological point of view the Pharisee's prayer is quite correct. It avoids pride by praising God for his grace in giving the Pharisee a totally different disposition toward life and the religious virtues of Judaism. Those listening to the parable for the first time might indeed have been totally misled into thinking the prayer is fine.

The publican's prayer, followed in quick order by the question of who went home justified, turns the issue in a very skillful way. Note that we are not asked whose prayer was good and whose bad, but whose prayer resulted in forgiveness: clearly the prayer of the publican.

Given the above setting, we must be careful to avoid the generalizing moralism in v. 14b. Pride in itself is not bad. It is the pride which leads to despising others which is under attack. Because v. 14b omits the idea of despising others, many have taken this as a secondary interpretation.[41] This verse suggests an eschatological reversal of fortunes, God will exalt the humble. The parable is about God who forgives those who ask for forgiveness.

Presenting the prophetic meaning. The major stress ought to be on the way even a theologically correct prayer can express contempt for others. We have heard the prayer, "There, but for the grace of God, go I." This is not as bad as the Pharisee's prayer in this parable, but it still contains the condescension against which Jesus speaks so strongly.

If we are going to be prophetic in the use of this parable we must be certain that we strike to the heart of the matter, which is the exclusivist attitude. Even though this attitude be clothed in the finest of emotions and words it is to be exposed. The more subtle the exclusivism, the harder it is to detect. The prophetic

41. So Linnemann, *op. cit.,* p. 64; Beare, *op. cit.,* p. 189; Jeremias is in doubt about v. 14b, *op. cit.,* p. 144, n. 62.

use of this great story even lays bare exclusivism within the camp of the holy ones, just as Jesus did in his day. This parable is aimed at the religious insiders, even if they have been condemning the Pharisees for two thousand years. As Paul put it, "What have I to do with judging outsiders? Is it not those inside the church whom you are to judge?" (1 Cor. 5:12). It is therefore clear that the prophetic interpretation does not allow one to move away from the specific situation to a general meaning, but rather to move from the original situation to one which is analogous in our time.

23. Parallel 190: The Parable of the Generous Employer—Matt. 20:1–16

Reconstructing the prophetic situation. If the previous parable may have had considerable force in its first hearing, the present one takes on added dynamics in afterthought or in retelling. The dynamics speed up when the laborers are paid at the end of the day. Vv. 8–10 follow in rapid succession: the householder instructs the paymaster to reverse the paying process by starting with the last; the one-hour laborers receive one denarius; at the end of the line come the twelve-hour laborers who expect to be paid more than all the rest. From that scene the plot is shifted. The last five verses represent the concluding conversation between the twelve-hour laborers and the householder. What needs to happen in rethinking the dynamics is to see the humorous situation in the parade of the payline. The first workers, the one-hour men, pass by and get their denarius. Nothing is said, but the three-, six-, and nine-hour workers also receive a denarius. The twelve-hour workers view this whole process and as they come up for their pay expect more than all the rest. They had of course been silent when all the rest of the workers were treated with equality. If the one-, three-, six-, and nine-hour laborers had all received a denarius they should have had no expectation of more. Their complaint ought to have been made sooner, at the point when the three-hour laborers got only one denarius. Had they acted then the cause would have been social justice. As it happens they are unconcerned about the fact that the one-, three-, six-, and nine-hour workers are treated equally. They are therefore placing themselves in a special category. They are the original group, charter members so to speak. The humor is that their selfishness is so transparent as to void their case for more pay. In response to such unsophisticated selfishness we could expect the householder to reply with scorn. Instead there is firmness. The householder speaks of his right to control what is his, and to be generous if he chooses.

Beare and Jeremias see the parable as a rebuke to those who protested the opening of the kingdom of God to the undeserving.[42] There is a good deal of sense in this, but the concentration of the parable is with the original laborers, not with the last who receive more than they have merited. When he says that this is a parable about grace not merit, Jeremias is dogmatizing the point. The message is directed against the original workers. The parable might have been spoken against

42. See Beare, *op. cit.*, p. 196, and Jeremias, *op. cit.*, p. 139.

the original disciples or the Jews, as the original people of God. The point is not that God is all grace, but how pathetic it is with the first disciples who want to have a special place, even when everyone else is considered equal.

Presenting the prophetic meaning. It is necessary to keep our presentation of this parable from being heavy on condemnation or on making too much about what God is like. We do not even know whether Jesus is referring to God, or to himself and his ministry. What is happening? The original elite are being confronted with their ambition to be extra special. Here is the pathology of the "charter member." It is crucial to use the parable situationally. It is not enough to say to the people of God, "God is grace." The charter members in the churches will still say, "Yes, God is grace, but remember we were first." This parable was designed to be prophetic in that situation.

(We of course wish to point out that we have paid scant if any attention to the stereotyped expression in v. 16.)

24. Parallel 203: The Parable of the Two Sons— Matt. 21:28–32

Reconstructing the prophetic situation. There is a debate as to whether v. 32 is original. I think it is, and agree with Beare. This parable was probably spoken at the beginning of the ministry of Jesus when the ministry of John the Baptist was still a major factor. Jesus is pointing to the reaction to John. The righteous people in the community have been standoffish. John has drawn his following from the morally undesirables ("tax collectors and harlots").[43] The point is that those in the community who are openly rebellious may in the long run turn out to be the ones who come through with the most for God and goodness.

Presenting the prophetic meaning. This is a very suggestive theme not usually found in most religious literature. The common way of looking at rebellion in society is to view it as a negative factor. We want "Mama's boy" to enter the ministry. He after all went to the synagogue and Sunday school with faithfulness! For Jesus rebellion is not as serious as lack of performance. He saw very deeply into the dynamics which exist in the family where the child who is the rebel may in reality be struggling with very important issues of identity which in the end will allow him to be creative and productive. Are we willing to work with the strong-minded types who may well say no to many things? Or do we need only yes men in the church? Presenting this parable as an important indicator about what was involved in the ministry of Jesus ought prophetically to force us to face this issue.

25. Parallel 204: The Parable of the Wicked Husbandman—Mark 12:1–12/Matt. 21:33–46/Luke 20:9–19/Thomas 65

Reconstructing the prophetic situation. It is important to note the parable as it occurs in the Gospel of Thomas:

---

43. In the debate about the originality of v. 32, Beare is for it, Beare, *op. cit.,* p. 208, and Jeremias against, *op. cit.,* p. 80.

A good man had a vineyard; he gave it to farmers that they might till it and he might receive its fruit from them. He sent his slave so that the farmers might give him the fruit of the vineyard. They overpowered his slave (and) beat him. They all but killed him. The slave came (and) told it to his master. His master said, "Perhaps he did not know them." He sent another slave; the famers beat the other. Then the master sent his son. He said, "Perhaps they will reverence my son." Since those farmers knew that he was the heir of the vineyard, they seized him (and) killed him. . . .[44]

To make a long story short, the version in the Gospel of Thomas looks like a more original version of the parable than any of the versions in the New Testament. The tendency in the New Testament is to allegorize the story so that the vineyard reminds us of Isaiah 5 where God has planted the vineyard, Israel (so the Matthean and Lucan versions—Mark does not have this detail). The son is also allegorized into Jesus and the death becomes the crucifixion. Matthew's is the most allegorical version, while Luke and Mark reflect the simplicity of Thomas in various ways. If one were preaching on one of the New Testament versions then Luke or Mark would be better than Matthew. Thomas would work too.

If we reconstruct the situation, Jesus is likely speaking to the people in his day about the fact that the

---

44. This is the translation of William Schoedel in Robert Grant and Noel Freedman's edition of the Gospel of Thomas, *The Secret Sayings of Jesus* (New York: Doubleday, 1960), pp. 171–72 (Thomas 66 in this numbering as opposed to the numbering used by Jeremias and the parallel headings in this study).

prophets and other messengers of God sent to them were shamefully treated. This may mean that judgment is near. Of course, the death of Jesus fits into this pattern, but it is important to recognize that Jesus himself is probably not responsible for all the details in the canonical versions. That was the work of the early church.

Presenting the prophetic meaning. It would be helpful to keep the message of this parable simple: the people of God often treat the messengers from God with shame and anger. The important point is not that once in history Jesus was rejected and killed, but rather that Jesus himself saw this going on in the whole of the history of the chosen people. We ought also to see that this type of action has continued in the history of Christianity. Those who bring truth from God are often rejected. Again, the presentation of this parable is helped if this type of activity is made concrete in the situation of the modern church. It is important to keep our presentation open-ended and to be on the alert at all times against any attack on the authentically prophetic voice.

26. *Parallel 205: The Parable of the Great Supper —Matt. 22:1–14/Luke 14:16–24/Thomas 64*

Reconstructing the prophetic situation. The situation of this parable is similar to the preceding one with one variation. In the Gospel of Thomas there is a gnostic ending which suggests that tradesmen and merchants do not enter the kingdom of God. With that exception, the version in the Gospel of Thomas seems to represent the most original version. This is another example of how important the 1945 discovery of the noncanonical manuscripts at Nag Hammadi, Egypt, has become to research on the Gospels. The suspicion of Jülicher that the allegorizing tendencies are later additions to the parables has been borne out in the Gospel of Thomas where most of its parables occur without allegory.

If vv. 22 and 23 are removed from the Lucan text we are probably in the presence of the version closest to the original form. These two verses seem to be an allegorical addition which attempts to bring the Gentile mission of the early church into the mission of Jesus. It also has the servants jumping the gun on the master with respect to inviting others to the banquet, a rather presumptuous action. Apart from this minor allegorizing, however, the Lucan version of the parable provides us with a good base for exploring the meaning of Jesus.

It is also most important to note that the Matthean version has considerably more allegory and interpretation which is not necessarily of much help in understanding the parable. To begin with, in Matthew the man giving the feast is a king, and he is giving the feast for his son. That is not too bad, but the allegory seems to point to the last judgment in an exclusive way, thus limiting the parable's meaning to an admonition for readiness for death.

More serious is the alteration of Matthew in v. 5 where the refusal of those invited is expressed with the words, "But they made light of it and went off, one to his farm, another to his business." This alteration in the text oversimplifies the situation into a black and white issue. There are those who take the invitation seriously and those who "make light of it." We shall show that there is more to the problem than this.

Another allegorizing addition in Matthew is the inclusion of an allegorical reference to the destruction of Jerusalem in vv. 6 and 7. Is it helpful to have the destruction of Jerusalem by Roman soldiers seen as God's punishment of Judaism's unbelief? We suggest that this is not consistently found in Jesus' teaching.

The final Matthean expansion of the parable is in vv. 11–14 where a whole section is added to the story. It appears that Matthew and his school were offended by the universalist implications of the Lucan version of the story. The poor, maimed, blind, and lame are the riff-raff of the city, and distinctions need to be made when dealing with such people. Thus Matthew warns us that in such a nondescript crowd there will be both good and bad people (v. 10), and even though all were invited they need to pass the test of proper dress. They are not all dressed properly, so Matthew has the king act with speed to make certain that his banquet is graced by only the "proper" type of people. Matthew has cleaned up the heavenly banquet, but at the cost of making God appear arbitrary, a great price indeed. Some have suggested, with merit, that it might be better to consider this last section as a separate parable.

All of this refers us back to the version in Luke. There we see simply the banquet and the invitation of three friends. They may well have been invited in advance and are now being given the final summons to the banquet, the food now being ready.[45] The refusals to come are, of course, put in correct speech, and they seem compelling. There is thus an element of sarcasm in Jesus' point: there is nothing wrong with the excuses being offered, it is just that the feast is ready.

The occasion for this parable is an analysis of the delayed response to Jesus' ministry. He may be pointing out that the Pharisees and the religious establishment have been given the invitation but have not taken it up, therefore he is turning in desperation to the sinners and outcasts of society. It should not be taken as a general condemnation of the religious of his day, but rather as a statement to those who have received a specific call to action. This is important, for not every moment in history is of equal importance. Not every call to action requires total and unqualified response. But when moments come which do demand such a response, we must be ready to drop all other matters. The men who refused thought there would be another day and another banquet, but they were wrong. The prophetic aspect of this is the requirement that men be aware of "the time" at every given moment of history.

Presenting the prophetic meaning. To insist that we must be constantly on tiptoe and at the beck and call of God and the church would be to generalize the parable. This can lead to the baptism of an attitude where Chris-

---

45. Jeremias points to the custom of first inviting, and then giving notice that the food is finally ready, so the feast can start. See Jeremias, *op. cit.,* p. 176.

tians become God's little firemen answering everything with equal speed and with full force—false alarm and five-alarm fires alike. This interpretation would also be in conflict with the parable of the two sons, where the one son did say no but later changed his mind and went.

What is in need of preservation is the reminder that decisive moments do exist when the banquet invitation is sent out and that the invitation must be answered at once. Again, the message has a situational aspect to it, and this also means that prophetic interpretation of it will have to discern when such decisive moments come in our generation. As Jesus said on another occasion, we are able to read the signs of the weather—we ought also to read the signs of God. What are the invitations being given to man and the church? Which of these invitations to life and action are of the decisive nature which demands immediate response?

27. Parallel 222: The Parable of the Doorkeeper —Mark 13:33–37 / Luke 12:35–38 (also Matt. 25:14–15b)

Reconstructing the prophetic situation. This is a parable which is only partially preserved in Matthew, and there is, furthermore, also a question of whether Mark or Luke preserves the more original form. Beare seems to think the Lucan version is more original, Jeremias the Marcan, and Bultmann sees the original parable in Mark 13:34 only, where the admonition to watch is directed to the doorkeepers in the community who assume this task for everyone.[46] Jeremias has taken elements from both the Marcan and Lucan versions in an attempt to reconstruct an original parable. His reconstruction follows Luke in having the man only go out for the evening to a banquet, but otherwise follows v. 34 in Mark: "We are then left with a core which consists of the parable of the Doorkeeper, who had received the command to keep watch (Mark 13:34b), and to open immediately as soon as his master, on his return from the banquet, should knock (Luke 12:36). It would be well for him if his master should find him watching, at whatever watch of the night he might return (Luke 12:37a, 38; Mark 13:35 f.)."[47] This represents an attempt to set the parable in the ministry of Jesus and to change the theme from watching for the return of Jesus at the end of time, to watching for the moment of God in the history of Israel. The scribes claimed to be the watchdogs of Israel, and Jesus is seen as addressing them about their function.[48]

Presenting the prophetic meaning. The church in reinterpreting this for the Christian situation still stresses the role of watching for God to be a community function, applying to at least some in the community in a very special way. Such an application is surely not out of line with the original intent of the parable.

Jeremias's reconstruction of the parable helps for the presentation of the parable to new situations. This par-

46. See Beare, *op. cit.,* p. 217; Jeremias, *op. cit.,* p. 54; Bultmann, *op. cit.,* p. 174.
47. Jeremias, *op. cit.,* p. 55.
48. Ibid.

able can be individualized to such an extreme that to live as a Christian and a religious person is at all times to play the game of consciously expecting that the present moment may be the very last moment for life and history. We can overextend ourselves on the watching theme. In Mark, not every servant is to be a watcher, but the whole community is to choose a doorkeeper and he is not to sleep. He is to awaken the whole community at the time of return. It is essential to make watchfulness one element in, but not the whole of, the Christian message. If we think of this in terms of Paul's idea of the body, then we see that the community has members with many differing functions. Jesus' message was not one to press everyone and everything into one mold. Some who have followed Jesus and rigidly interpreted his intent have ended with such an ideal of uniformity. However, to follow the prophetic emphasis in this parable does not mean that every man is to be a prophet or doorkeeper. It does mean that those looking for the time of action are to stay watchful and be awake at the right time.

28. Parallel 226: The Parable of the Servant Entrusted with Supervision—Matt. 24:45–51/ Luke 12:42–46

Reconstructing the prophetic situation. Here is another parable which seems to be set in the situation of the parousia of Christ. This is not a bad vantage point from which to translate the parable, but it is not the original setting. The original parable is of a servant who was entrusted with the estate, and when the master was gone he began to abuse those placed under him. Then the master returns unexpectedly and punishes the servant. In the ministry of Jesus this probably represents a criticism of the scribes and the rest of the religious establishment which has been entrusted with the care of the house of Israel. Their trust has been violated by selfishness. Jesus is saying that their day of reckoning is not far off: God will come and they will be caught in their selfishness.

Presenting the prophetic meaning. The stress here is on the responsibility given the leaders in the religious community, and on their tendency to confuse that position of responsibility with one of privilege. Jesus is only saying that the religious community is not different from the secular society in this respect. Those who would like to assume that the leaders of the religious society are somehow more exempt from worldly temptations of power will find that Jesus does not share their idealism. This parable suggests that we must be on our guard in respect to our religious society in the same way we are on guard against what might happen in the political field in general. Favoritism, power politics, and the rest can be present in the religious community. To those who like to feel that the religious community is not to be looked at like any other community, this parable stands as firm warning. We can use this parable prophetically only to the extent that we are willing to face up to the present pathology of the church and all institutions of religion, making our criticism in honesty. There is indeed a great deal of truth in what is being said in current study about the pathology of institutions. "The establishment" can very easily be self-serving when it ought to be responsible. The prophet again has to learn to laugh at his own religious organization and even at himself if he stands in a position of favor in the organization. He is not called to be totally negative about organization but to be totally realistic.

29. Parallel 227: The Parable of the Ten Maidens —Matt. 25:1–13

Reconstructing the prophetic situation. There is general agreement concerning the allegorical form of this parable. We have seen Matthew adding allegorical detail to other parables, for example, the parable of the great banquet. The story of the ten maidens has been made into an allegory of the second coming of Christ, where he is the bridegroom. The delay of his arrival is the delay of the parousia. The ten maidens are the Christian community and the separation of the wise from the foolish is the last judgment. If we wish to take recent studies into account we must thus look behind Matthew's allegorical statement of the parable.[49]

Here we will find a division of scholarly opinion. Beare holds that the parable is a reworking of the parable of the doorkeeper, and therefore not a parable

---

49. A few of the recent studies which speak of the Matthean allegorizing are: Dan O. Via, Jr., *The Parables, Their Literary and Existential Dimension* (Philadelphia: Fortress Press, 1967), pp. 123–24; Beare, *op. cit.,* pp. 217–18; Jeremias, *op. cit.,* pp. 51–52.

which goes back to Jesus.[50] Jeremias presents another way of looking at the question by redirecting the situation into the life of Jesus. The parable then points to a sudden moment of crisis when only half are truly prepared.[51]

Jesus must indeed have been pointing to some moment of crisis. What that was we cannot know. There was, however, a particular situational dynamic which he wanted to highlight; he wanted to show that there was a division in his community. The group of maidens represents a community which was for all purposes united in waiting for a great event. They were united, that is, until the event arrived, then the division became apparent. All ten, the whole community, were equally watchful. The issue is not that five went to sleep and five stayed awake. The issue is rather that five of the young ladies somehow assumed that oil would always be available, or they could quickly buy more, or the door of the wedding feast would always swing open to them.

The arrival of the bridegroom need not be the final judgment. The closing of the door need not be final damnation. Still, there is a quality of sternness to the point Jesus is making: it is not enough just to be along for the ride. Preparation and serious participation are part of life in the community. This is as far as we can go. What kind of serious preparation was involved is not known. Who the unprepared five were is also unknown. What we can see is a deadly serious call by

50. Beare, *op. cit.,* p. 218.
51. Jeremias, *op. cit.,* pp. 51–52.

120

Jesus for very responsible action. There is no humor in this situation. We could say, furthermore, that this parable lacks the sparkle of the authentic parables of Jesus, but that would be the easy way out. Jesus came proclaiming the new commandment of love, announcing the presence of the kingdom of God. However, love, joy, and celebration are not just for laughs, they are for real life. There are appropriate times for preparation, for waiting, for action, and for celebration.

Presenting the prophetic meaning. This is a difficult parable if we want to be specific about its meaning. The original situation is so hidden in the shadows that we do not possess the kind of clarity we might like. We can, of course, raise the question of the breadth of Jesus' total response to life and people. In his total preaching humor and sternness were not mutually self-exclusive.

We have, further, the question of distinguishing between the dilettante and the worker. This question, however, must be presented with no reversion to self-righteousness. That is where seriousness and humor have to go together, and we need a special measure of grace to make such a presentation.

30. Parallel 228: The Parable of the Talents— Matt. 25:14–30 / Luke 19:12–27

Reconstructing the prophetic situation. This parable and its two versions confront us with what hopefully has become a useful exercise in the course of the present study. The task is to work at the reconstruction of the

121

simple story without allegorical embellishments or secondary interpretations. In general, the Matthean version seems to be the better version especially if the parable is seen as stopping at 25:27 or possibly at v. 28. We have a story of a man giving three servants three different sums of money. At his return he finds that two had invested it and made profits, and one had buried his treasure in the field where no increase in value would be received. The phrase, "enter into the joy of your master," may have been secondary, a phrase possibly added to turn the reference of the parable to the heavenly reward at the end of the age. It also may be that all three servants were given an equal sum of money, and not as much as a "talent." These additions to the Matthean version, however, do not greatly alter the version.

In Luke we see many other issues introduced into the parable. It would be well, therefore, to turn to the long discussions of Luke's alterations in Jeremias and Beare. What the Lucan version turns out to be is a parable about Jesus' ascension as an "enthronement" journey. He gave each of ten servants a mina (about twenty dollars). Two of the ten invested and were rewarded for the returns they earned, one did not and was punished. There is also a story about those who opposed the enthronement and who killed the nobleman on his return because of their opposition to his enthronement. These possibilities are confusing, but they point to the type of reconstruction which can be made from the Matthean account.[52]

52. See Beare, *op. cit.*, pp. 201 ff., and Jeremias, *op. cit.*, pp. 58 ff.

The occasion is not the last judgment, but is rather a comment by Jesus concerning the religious attitudes of his day. He points to the fact that most anyone would be able to see the logic of investment and risk in the life of business, but that these same people fail to take any risk in religious life. This is the ironic contradiction in the life of his people and in the lives of many individuals in his community. The treasure given them is not put to use, but hoarded in the ground where it is of no use to anyone. We see the parable as a word directed against the caution of the religious establishment in Jesus' day. They had a great gift in their heritage but were hiding it, and preserving it by keeping it to themselves. To hide the gift was not to have it.

Presenting the prophetic meaning. We have to be careful that we do not use this parable as Luke did so as to affirm an anti-Semitic attitude. Jesus was not anti-Semitic, but anti-establishment. That means he was against any religious establishment which would become defensive and negative, an attitude reflected in the remarks of the third servant. He was afraid, and he hid the treasure to protect it. To direct a prophetic message toward this type of negative and defensive attitude is very often needed in the life of the church. In all religious traditions there is a temptation to become introverted and defensive. Jesus is here saying that risk in the religious dimensions of life is not much different from risk in the world of business. He is not baptizing the capitalistic system, say, but rather pointing out that capitalists and all men alike ought to be as daring in religion as they are in business. This means that we must be willing to have a positive attitude toward ourselves, God, and the future. Prophecy here is not just to criticize, but to inspire to action.

31. Parallel 229: The Parable of the Last Judgment—Matt. 25:31–45

Reconstructing the prophetic situation. The debate about this parable's authenticity is extensive. Bultmann and others have argued that this was not spoken by Jesus, but is rather a piece of traditional Jewish apocalyptic about the final judgment.[53] A further argument against its authenticity is the titles of majesty which are applied to Jesus. To call Jesus Son of man and also King in the heavenly last judgment sounds more like the early church than Jesus himself. However, these arguments are not as weighty as they might appear on first examination.

The point of the parable does not demand that Jesus be judge. We might well assume that the early church made this identification. Jesus could be describing how it will be when God judges us at the end of the age.

More important is the observation of Jeremias that this is not a typical judgment story insofar as the righteous are surprised at being among the saved.[54] The religious community can often look at the last judgment in respect to the unrighteous, but the righteous are not normally surprised. They are, in contrast, usually happy that at long last God has finally vindi-

53. So Bultmann, *op. cit.*, pp. 123–24, and Beare, *op. cit.*, pp. 218–19.
54. Jeremias, *op. cit.*, p. 208.

cated their cause. The religious community often looks at the last judgment without humor. They assume that they are on the side of God. This parable thus clearly breaks the normal pattern of the morality story. The humor in it is the surprised reaction of both the righteous and the unrighteous. Further, there is surprise in that they have confronted their judge in the midst of the poor and wretched of the world. The story is not didactic but prophetic. It does not teach new understandings of morality, but presses for sensitivity to the situations of life in which the poor are confronted.

Because there is so much surprise in the parable we can only conclude that Jesus was combating a very moralistic view both of life and the judgment of God. He could well have found this moralism among the Pharisees. His point is that it is not possible to reduce life to a set of do's and don'ts. The popular understanding of morality common to the Pharisees and many others, needed expansion. If one is to move beyond the morality of the majority, one must be concerned with his brother (vv. 40, 45). Again we see Jesus reaching beyond legal requirements to see life in its totality and wholeness. Not just the important, but also the insignificant aspects of life count. Thus we can see Jesus struggling with the question of how God judges man and life. He wished to move beyond the usual picture of the righteous man who knows he is saved and stands before God with the same kind of self-centeredness as the Pharisees in the parable of the Pharisee and the publican. Against those who defined morality as the working out of general moral principles (God's law) in specific situations, Jesus comes with an extra factor of reality: that God is more than law giver. He is present himself in the world struggling with our brothers, and when we meet our brother, we meet God. This is the poetry of reality and radicality. This is also the meaning of life and love.

Presenting the prophetic meaning. How rigid are we as persons with a moral consciousness? Are there situations in our day where we act as though we can be our own judges of good and bad? This parable speaks a word of both judgment and hope to that situation. In judgment it says that being a moral crusader, or a famous liberal in your community is not the whole of the story. What do you do when you are not on stage? The condemned were self-righteous in their view of love, for they pointed out that they had never neglected the required works of charity. God's response is that they have passed their brother by many times. They must have been off stage at least part of the time, and when they were they did not act in a moral way. The faithful and blessed in the parable are the same kind of people—with a difference. They have an on-stage and an off-stage part of life too, but there was less play acting in their life. To them came a word of hope. They had done many good things when they were off stage; without calculation or even thinking about it they had given aid to their brothers. The point of the parable is more a vision of the last judgment. It is also a prophetic word about life. Not that faith must be followed up with a consciously worked out program of goodness (there is nothing wrong with that), but that faith is to open us up to a full and spontaneous life. When man is freed by God he is released into the totality of life and the fullness of God. What he does with the little moments and the little brothers is qualified by his freedom. Being free he can also liberate others. He is more than a do-gooder piling up "brownie points" for himself. He is more than the moralistic man, the missionary, or the white middle-class liberal—he is the man of freedom through faith.

In working through the implications of a prophetic interpretation of the parables we have stressed: attention to life's concrete situations, humor, and a wisdom which says that life should inform our religious attitudes. These factors provide insight into Jesus, who comes with an authority beyond that of the scribe and the Pharisee. These factors also carry us beyond interpretation to life.

THE PREACHER'S PAPERBACK LIBRARY

Volumes already published:

1. *The Servant of the Word* by H. H. Farmer. 1964.
2. *The Care of the Earth and Other University Sermons* by Joseph Sittler. 1964.
3. *The Preaching of F. W. Robertson* edited with an Introduction by Gilbert E. Doan, Jr. 1964.
4. *A Brief History of Preaching* by Yngve Brilioth. 1965.
5. *The Living Word* by Gustaf Wingren. 1965.
6. *On Prayer* by Gerhard Ebeling. 1966.
7. *Renewal in the Pulpit*—Sermons by Younger Preachers edited with an Introduction by Edmund A. Steimle. 1966.
8. *The Preaching of Chrysostom: Homilies on the Sermon on the Mount* edited with an Introduction by Jaroslav Pelikan. 1967.
9. *Violent Sleep*—Notes Toward the Development of Sermons for the Modern City by Richard Luecke. 1969.
10. *The Preaching of John Henry Newman* edited with an Introduction by W. D. White. 1969.

11. *Interpretation and Imagination*—The Preacher and Contemporary Literature by Charles L. Rice. 1970.

12. *Preaching On the Parables* by David M. Granskou. 1972.

Type, 11 on 13 and 10 on 11 Garamond
Display, Garamond